A Yorkshire Fable

Thirty knitting designs

Kim Hargreaves • Martin Storey • Sarah Dallas

Sasha Kagan • Sharon Peake • Muir & Osborne

Louisa Harding • Lucinda Guy • Sharon Miller

ROWAN

Copyright © Rowan Yarns 2003
First published in Great Britain in 2003 by
Rowan Yarns Ltd
Green Lane Mill
Holmfirth
West Yorkshire
England
HD9 2DX

Internet: www.knitrowan.com
Email: yorkshirefable@knitrowan.com

Designs & Styling Kim Hargreaves
Photographer Joey Toller
Front cover Hair & Make-up Liz Kitchener
Model Georgina Harrison
All other photographs Hair & Make-up Annabel Hobbs
Models Lauren Tempany, Irina Malakhova & Jake Thomson
Book Design Kim Hargreaves
Design Co-ordinator Stella Smith
Design Layout Les Dunford
Knitting co-ordinators Elizabeth Armitage & Michelle Moorhouse
Pattern writers Kathleen Hargreaves & Sue Whiting

British Library Cataloguing in Publication Data
Rowan Yarns
Yorkshire Fable
1. Knitting – patterns
1 Title
ISBN 1-904485-06-5

Printed by KHL Printing Co Pte Ltd
Singapore

Contents

Oakworth by Sarah Dallas

Home Sweet Home by Kim Hargreaves, Bronte scarf by Sharon Miller,
Joseph by Kim Hargreaves, Oakworth by Sarah Dallas and Mist hat by Kim Hargreaves

Cable Rose by Sasha Kagan

Breeze by Kim Hargreaves

Sailor Stripe and Mist hat both by Kim Hargreaves

Breeze and Willow by Kim Hargreaves

Kirkby by Marin Storey and Stocksmoor by Louisa Harding

Bobbie by Muir & Osborne and Mist hat by Kim Hargreaves

Hepworth & Bilberry both by Louisa Harding and Mist hat by Kim Hargreaves

Wispy by Kim Hargreaves

Honesty by Kim Hargreaves

Merry and Mist hat both by Kim Hargreaves

Perkins by Sarah Dallas and Miller by Kim Hargreaves

Jane and Mist hat by Kim Hargreaves

Kirkby by Martin Storey and Stocksmoor by Lousia Harding

Weatherby by Martin Storey

24

Renaissance by Kim Hargreaves

Moor by Kim Hargreaves

Windswept by Kim Hargreaves and Col by Sharon Peake

Charlotte by Kim Hargreaves

Windswept and Jess both by Kim Hargreaves

Miller by Kim Hargreaves

Ernest by Kim Hargreaves, Love Birds by Lucinda Guy and Mist hat by Kim Hargreaves

Moor by Kim Hargreaves

Tiny Flower by Sasha Kagan, Kirkby by Martin Storey,
Sampler and Mist hat both by Kim Hargreaves and Bronte scarf by Sharon Miller

Kirkby by Martin Storey

Sampler and Mist hat by Kim Hargreaves and Bronte scarf by Sharon Miller

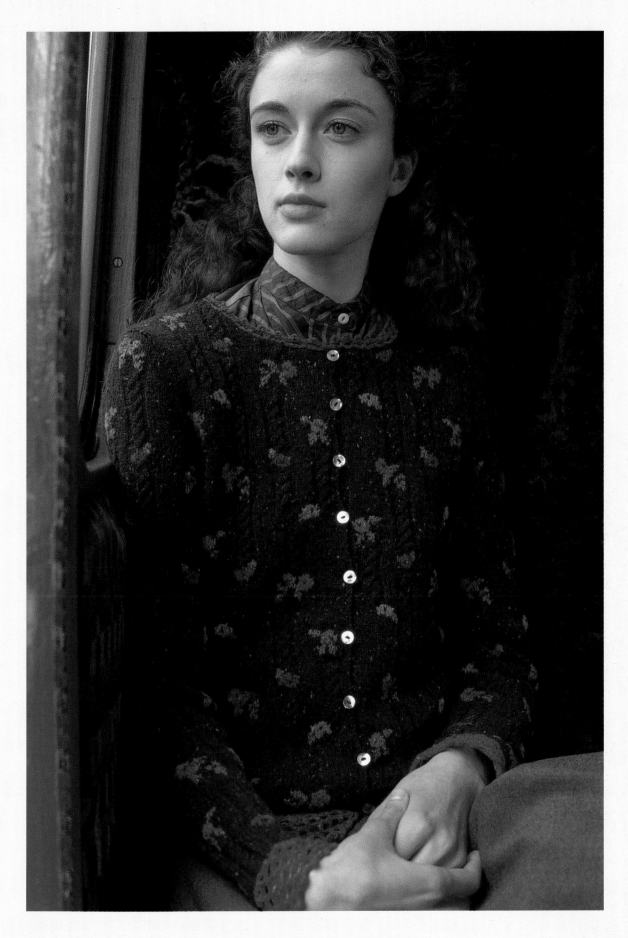

Tiny Flower by Sasha Kagan

Tiny Flower by Sasha Kagan, Kirkby by Martin Storey,
Sampler and Mist hat both by Kim Hargreaves and Bronte scarf by Sharon Miller

Love Birds by Lucinda Guy and Mist hat by Kim Hargreaves

Design number 1

JESS

KIM HARGREAVES

YARN

	XS	S	M	L	XL
To fit bust	81	86	91	97	102cm
	32	34	36	38	40 in

Rowan Yorkshire Tweed 4 ply

| | 10 | 11 | 12 | 12 | 13 x 25gm |

(photographed in Enchant 268)

NEEDLES

1 pair 2¾mm (no 12) (US 2) needles
1 pair 3¼mm (no 10) (US 3) needles
2.50mm (no 12) (US C2) crochet hook

TENSION

26 sts and 38 rows to 10 cm measured over stocking stitch using 3¼mm (US 3) needles.

CROCHET ABBREVIATIONS

Ss = slip stitch; **dc** = double crochet; **ch** = chain.

BACK

Cast on 111 (117: 123: 129: 135) sts using 2¾mm (US 2) needles.
Row 1 (RS): K1, *P1, K1, rep from * to end.
Row 2: P1, *K1, P1, rep from * to end.
These 2 rows form rib.
Cont in rib for a further 8 rows, ending with a WS row.
Change to 3¼mm (US 3) needles.
Beg with a K row, work in st st for 4 rows.
Cont in lace patt as folls:
Row 1 (RS): K6 (9: 12: 3: 6), *yfwd, sl 1, K2tog, psso, yfwd, K9, rep from * to last 9 (12: 15: 6: 9) sts, yfwd, sl 1, K2tog, psso, yfwd, K to end.
Row 2 and every foll alt row: Purl.
Row 3: K4 (7: 10: 1: 4), *K2tog, yfwd, K3, yfwd, sl 1, K1, psso, K5, rep from * to last 11 (14: 17: 8: 11) sts, K2tog, yfwd, K3, yfwd, sl 1, K1, psso, K to end.
Row 5: As row 1.
Row 7: Knit.
Row 9: K2tog, K10 (13: 4: 7: 10), *yfwd, sl 1, K2tog, psso, yfwd, K9, rep from * to last 15 (18: 9: 12: 15) sts, yfwd, sl 1, K2tog, psso, yfwd, K to last 2 sts, K2tog. 109 (115: 121: 127: 133) sts.

Row 11: K9 (12: 3: 6: 9), *K2tog, yfwd, K3, yfwd, sl 1, K1, psso, K5, rep from * to last 16 (19: 10: 13: 16) sts, K2tog, yfwd, K3, yfwd, sl 1, K1, psso, K to end.
Row 13: K2tog, K9 (12: 3: 6: 9), *yfwd, sl 1, K2tog, psso, yfwd, K9, rep from * to last 14 (17: 8: 11: 14) sts, yfwd, sl 1, K2tog, psso, yfwd, K to last 2 sts, K2tog. 107 (113: 119: 125: 131) sts.
Row 15: Knit.
Row 16: As row 2.
These 16 rows form first section of lace patt and start side seam shaping.
Work in lace patt for a further 16 rows, dec 1 st at each end of next and every foll 4th row and ending with a WS row.
99 (105: 111: 117: 123) sts.
Change to 2¾mm (US 2) needles.
Work in rib as given for lower edge for 24 rows, dec 1 st at each end of first of these rows and ending with a WS row. 97 (103: 109: 115: 121) sts.
Change to 3¼mm (US 3) needles.
Beg with a K row, work in st st for 4 rows, inc 1 st at each end of first of these rows.
99 (105: 111: 117: 123) sts.
Cont in lace patt as folls:
Row 1 (RS): K6 (9: 12: 3: 6), *yfwd, sl 1, K2tog, psso, yfwd, K9, rep from * to last 9 (12: 15: 6: 9) sts, yfwd, sl 1, K2tog, psso, yfwd, K to end.
Row 2 and every foll alt row: Purl.
Row 3: K4 (7: 10: 1: 4), *K2tog, yfwd, K3, yfwd, sl 1, K1, psso, K5, rep from * to last 11 (14: 17: 8: 11) sts, K2tog, yfwd, K3, yfwd, sl 1, K1, psso, K to end.
Row 5: As row 1.
Row 7: Inc in first st, K to last st, inc in last st.
101 (107: 113: 119: 125) sts.
Row 9: K13 (4: 7: 10: 13), *yfwd, sl 1, K2tog, psso, yfwd, K9, rep from * to last 16 (7: 10: 13: 16) sts, yfwd, sl 1, K2tog, psso, yfwd, K to end.
Row 11: K11 (2: 5: 8: 11), *K2tog, yfwd, K3, yfwd, sl 1, K1, psso, K5, rep from * to last 18 (9: 12: 15: 18) sts, K2tog, yfwd, K3, yfwd, sl 1, K1, psso, K to end.
Row 13: As row 11.
Row 15: Knit.
Row 16: As row 2.
These 16 rows form patt for rem of back and cont side seam shaping.
Cont in patt as now set, inc 1 st at each end of next and every foll 10th row until there are 111 (117: 123: 129: 135) sts, taking inc sts into patt.
Cont straight until back measures 37 (38: 38: 39: 39) cm, ending with a WS row.
Shape armholes
Keeping patt correct, cast off 5 (6: 6: 7: 7) sts at beg of next 2 rows. 101 (105: 111: 115: 121) sts.
Dec 1 st at each end of next 5 (5: 7: 7: 9) rows, then on foll 4 (5: 5: 6: 6) alt rows.
83 (85: 87: 89: 91) sts.
Cont straight until armhole measures 20 (20: 21: 21: 22) cm, ending with a WS row.
Shape shoulders and back neck
Cast off 7 sts at beg of next 2 rows.
69 (71: 73: 75: 77) sts.
Next row (RS): Cast off 7 sts, patt until there are 10 (10: 11: 11: 12) sts on right needle and turn, leaving rem sts on a holder.
Work each side of neck separately.
Cast off 4 sts at beg of next row.
Cast off rem 6 (6: 7: 7: 8) sts.
With RS facing, rejoin yarn to rem sts, cast off centre 35 (37: 37: 39: 39) sts, patt to end.
Complete to match first side, reversing shapings.

FRONT

Work as given for back until 22 (22: 22: 24: 24) rows less have been worked than on back to start of shoulder shaping, ending with a WS row.
Shape neck
Next row (RS): Patt 33 (33: 34: 35: 36) sts and turn, leaving rem sts on a holder.
Work each side of neck separately.
Dec 1 st at neck edge of next 10 rows, then on foll 3 (3: 3: 4: 4) alt rows. 20 (20: 21: 21: 22) sts.
Work 5 rows, ending with a WS row.
Shape shoulder
Cast off 7 sts at beg of next and foll alt row.
Work 1 row.
Cast off rem 6 (6: 7: 7: 8) sts.
With RS facing, rejoin yarn to rem sts, cast off centre 17 (19: 19: 19: 19) sts, patt to end.
Complete to match first side, reversing shapings.

SLEEVES (both alike)

Cast on 69 (69: 71: 73: 73) sts using 2¾mm (US 2) needles.
Work in rib as given for back for 26 rows, inc 1 st at each end of 25th of these rows and ending with a WS row. 71 (71: 73: 75: 75) sts.
Change to 3¼mm (US 3) needles.
Cont in lace patt as folls:
Row 1 (RS): Knit.
Row 2 and every foll alt row: Purl.
Row 3: K10 (10: 11: 12: 12), *yfwd, sl 1, K2tog, psso, yfwd, K9, rep from * to last 13 (13: 14: 15: 15) sts, yfwd, sl 1, K2tog, psso, yfwd, K to end.
Row 5: K8 (8: 9: 10: 10), *K2tog, yfwd, K3, yfwd, sl 1, K1, psso, K5, rep from * to last 15 (15: 16: 17: 17) sts, K2tog, yfwd, K3, yfwd, sl 1, K1, psso, K to end.
Row 7: As row 3.
Row 9: (Inc in first st) 0 (1: 0: 0: 1) times, K to last 0 (1: 0: 0: 1) st, (inc in last st) 0 (1: 0: 0: 1) times. 71 (73: 73: 75: 77) sts.
Row 11: (Inc in first st) 1 (0: 1: 1: 0) times, K3 (5: 4: 5: 7), *yfwd, sl 1, K2tog, psso, yfwd, K9, rep from * to last 7 (8: 8: 9: 10) sts, yfwd, sl 1, K2tog, psso, yfwd, K to last 1 (0: 1: 1: 0) st, (inc in last st) 1 (0: 1: 1: 0) times.
73 (73: 75: 77: 77) sts.
Row 13: K3 (3: 4: 5: 5), *K2tog, yfwd, K3, yfwd, sl 1, K1, psso, K5, rep from * to last 10 (10: 11: 12: 12) sts, K2tog, yfwd, K3, yfwd, sl 1, K1, psso, K to end.
Row 15: K5 (5: 6: 7: 7), *yfwd, sl 1, K2tog, psso, yfwd, K9, rep from * to last 8 (8: 9: 10: 10) sts, yfwd, sl 1, K2tog, psso, yfwd, K to end.
Row 16: As row 2.
These 16 rows form patt and start sleeve shaping.
Cont in patt, inc 1 st at each end of 7th (3rd: 7th: 7th: 3rd) and every foll 12th (10th: 10th: 10th: 10th) row to 81 (95: 97: 99: 95) sts, then on every foll 10th (-: -: -: 8th) row to 93 (-: -: -: 101) sts, taking inc sts into patt.
Cont straight until sleeve measures 43 (43: 44: 44: 44) cm, ending with a WS row.
Shape top
Keeping patt correct, cast off 5 (6: 6: 7: 7) sts at beg of next 2 rows. 83 (83: 85: 85: 87) sts.
Dec 1 st at each end of next 5 rows, then on foll 3 alt rows, then on every foll 4th row until 51 (51: 53: 53: 55) sts rem.
Work 1 row.
Dec 1 st at each end of next and every foll alt row until 47 sts rem, then on foll 5 rows, ending with a WS row. 37 sts.
Cast off 5 sts at beg of next 2 rows.
Cast off rem 27 sts.

MAKING UP

PRESS as described on the information page. Join right shoulder seam using back stitch, or mattress st if preferred.

Neckband

With RS facing and using 3¼mm (US 3) needles, pick up and knit 26 (26: 26: 28: 28) sts down left side of neck, 17 (19: 19: 19: 19) sts from front, 26 (26: 26: 28: 28) sts up right side of neck, then 44 (46: 46: 48: 48) sts from back. 113 (117: 117: 123: 123) sts.
Work in rib as given for back for 1.5 cm.
Cast off in rib.
See information page for finishing instructions, setting in sleeves using the set-in method.

Crochet edging

With RS facing and using 2.50mm (US C2) crochet hook, work 1 round of dc evenly around neck edge, working an even number of sts and ending with ss to first dc.
Next round: 1 ch (does NOT count as st), 1 dc into first dc, *3 ch, 1 dc into same place as last dc★★, 1 dc into each of next 2 dc, rep from ★ to end, ending last rep at ★★, 1 dc into next dc, ss to first dc.
Fasten off.
Work crochet edging around lower edge of sleeves in same way.

57 (58: 59: 60: 61) cm
(22.5 (23: 23: 23.5: 24) in)

42.5 (45: 47.5: 49.5: 52) cm
(16.5 (17.5: 18.5: 19.5: 20.5) in)

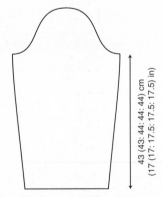

43 (43: 44: 44: 44) cm
(17 (17: 17.5: 17.5: 17.5) in)

Design number 2

MOOR

KIM HARGREAVES

YARN

	ladies			mens			
	S	M	L	M	L	XL	
To fit bust/chest	86	91	97	102	107	112	cm
	34	36	38	40	42	44	in

Rowan Yorkshire Tweed 4 ply

Multi coloured version

A Cheerful	271	3	3	4	5	5	6	x 25gm
B Lustre	282	2	2	2	2	2	2	x 25gm
C Graze	286	2	2	2	2	3	3	x 25gm
D B'scotch	272	2	2	2	3	3	3	x 25gm
E Glory	273	1	1	1	1	1	1	x 25gm
F Brilliant	274	1	1	1	1	1	1	x 25gm
G Foxy	275	1	1	1	1	1	1	x 25gm
H Deep Aub.	280	1	1	1	1	1	1	x 25gm

Four coloured version

A Whiskers	283	3	3	4	4	5	5	x 25gm
B Explode	277	2	2	2	3	3	3	x 25gm
C Stainless	270	2	2	2	2	2	2	x 25gm
D Desiccated	263	3	3	3	4	4	5	x 25gm

NEEDLES

1 pair 2¾mm (no 12) (US 2) needles
1 pair 3¼mm (no 10) (US 3) needles

TENSION

30 sts and 35 rows to 10 cm measured over patterned stocking stitch using 3¼mm (US 3) needles.

Pattern note: The pattern is written for the 3 ladies sizes, followed by the mens sizes in **bold**. Where only one figure appears this applies to all sizes in that group.

BACK

Cast on 123 (131: 139: **145: 153: 161**) sts using 2¾mm (US 2) needles and yarn C (**B**).
Break off yarn C (**B**) and join in yarn A.
Row 1 (RS): K1, *P1, K1, rep from ★ to end.
Row 2: P1, ★K1, P1, rep from ★ to end.
These 2 rows form rib.
Cont in rib until back measures 6.5 (**8**) cm, ending with a WS row.
Change to 3¼mm (US 3) needles.
Using the **fairisle** technique as described on the information page, starting and ending rows as indicated and repeating the 42 row pattern repeat throughout, cont in patt from appropriate chart as folls:
Inc 1 st at each end of 3rd and every foll 10th (**12th**) row until there are 137 (145: 153: **161: 169: 177**) sts, taking inc sts into patt.
Cont straight until back measures 28 (29: 30: **40: 41: 42**) cm, ending with a WS row.

Shape armholes

Keeping patt correct, cast off 6 (7: 8: **8: 9: 10**) sts at beg of next 2 rows.
125 (131: 137: **145: 151: 157**) sts.
Dec 1 st at each end of next 5 (**7**) rows, then on foll 7 (**6**) alt rows.
101 (107: 113: **119: 125: 131**) sts.
Cont straight until armhole measures 20 (21: 22: **23: 24: 25**) cm, ending with a WS row.

Shape shoulders and back neck

Cast off 9 (9: 10: **10: 11: 11**) sts at beg of next 2 rows. 83 (89: 93: **99: 103: 109**) sts.
Next row (RS): Cast off 9 (9: 10: **10: 11: 11**) sts, patt until there are 13 (14: 13: **15: 14: 15**) sts on right needle and turn, leaving rem sts on a holder.
Work each side of neck separately.
Cast off 4 sts at beg of next row.
Cast off rem 9 (10: 9: **11: 10: 11**) sts.
With RS facing, rejoin yarns to rem sts, cast off centre 39 (43: 47: **49: 53: 57**) sts, patt to end.
Complete to match first side, reversing shapings.

FRONT

Work as given for back until 22 (**26**) rows less have been worked than on back to start of shoulder shaping, ending with a WS row.

Shape neck

Next row (RS): Patt 40 (41: 42: **46: 47: 48**) sts and turn, leaving rem sts on a holder.
Work each side of neck separately.
Dec 1 st at neck edge of next 8 (**10**) rows, then on foll 5 alt rows. 27 (28: 29: **31: 32: 33**) sts.
Work 3 (**5**) rows, ending with a WS row.

Shape shoulder

Cast off 9 (9: 10: **10: 11: 11**) sts at beg of next and foll alt row.
Work 1 row.
Cast off rem 9 (10: 9: **11: 10: 11**) sts.
With RS facing, rejoin yarns to rem sts, cast off centre 21 (25: 29: **27: 31: 35**) sts, patt to end.
Complete to match first side, reversing shapings.

MAKING UP

PRESS as described on the information page.

Join right shoulder seam using back stitch, or mattress st if preferred.

Neckband

With RS facing, using 2¾mm (US 2) needles and yarn A, pick up and knit 26 (**30**) sts down left side of neck, 21 (25: 29: **27: 31: 35**) sts from front, 26 (**30**) sts up right side of neck, then 48 (52: 56: **58: 62: 66**) sts from back.
121 (129: 137: **145: 153: 161**) sts.
Work in rib as given for back for 7 (**9**) rows.
Break off yarn A and join in yarn C (**B**).

Work in rib for 1 row more. Cast off in rib.
Join left shoulder and neckband seam.

Armhole borders (both alike)

With RS facing, using 2¾mm (US 2) needles and yarn A, pick up and knit 131 (139: 147: **155: 163: 171**) sts.
Work in rib as given for back for 7 (**9**) rows.
Break off yarn A and join in yarn C (**B**).
Work in rib for 1 row more.
Cast off in rib.
See information page for finishing instructions.

48 (50: 52: **63: 65: 67**) cm
(19 (19.5: 20.5: **25: 25.5: 26.5**) in)

45.5 (48.5: 51: **53.5: 56.5: 59**) cm
(18 (19: 20: **21: 22: 23**) in)

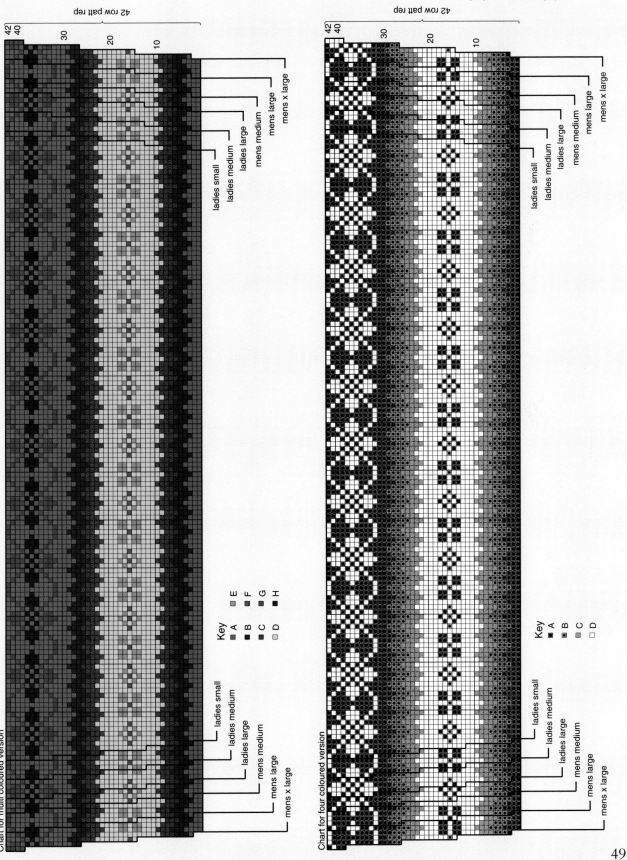

Design number 3

WETHERBY

MARTIN STOREY

YARN

	S	M	L	XL	XXL
To fit chest	97	102	107	112	117 cm
	38	40	42	44	46 in

Rowan Magpie

| | 10 | 11 | 11 | 12 | 12 x 100gm |

(photographed in Tranquil 689)

NEEDLES

1 pair 4mm (no 8) (US 6) needles
1 pair 5mm (no 6) (US 8) needles
Cable needle

TENSION

18 sts and 23 rows to 10 cm measured over stocking stitch using 5mm (US 8) needles.

SPECIAL ABBREVIATIONS

Cr4L = Cross 4 left Slip next 3 sts onto cn and leave at front of work, P1, then K3 from cn
Cr4R = Cross 4 right Slip next st onto cn and leave at back of work, K3, then P1 from cn
C6B = Cable 6 back Slip next 3 sts onto cn and leave at back of work, K3, then K3 from cn
Cr8L = Cross 8 left Slip next 6 sts onto cn and leave at front of work, P2, then K6 from cn
Cr8R = Cross 8 right Slip next 2 sts onto cn and leave at back of work, K6, then P2 from cn
C11B = Cable 11 back Slip next 6 sts onto cn and leave at back of work, (K1 tbl, P1) twice, K1 tbl, then (P1, K1 tbl) 3 times from cn
C12B = Cable 12 back Slip next 6 sts onto cn and leave at back of work, K6, then K6 from cn
C12F = Cable 12 front Slip next 6 sts onto cn and leave at front of work, K6, then K6 from cn

BACK

Cast on 103 (107: 111: 115: 119) sts using 4mm (US 6) needles.
Row 1 (RS): K0 (1: 0: 0: 1), P2 (3: 0: 2: 3), ★K3, P3, rep from ★ to last 5 (1: 3: 5: 1) sts, K3 (1: 3: 3: 1), P2 (0: 0: 2: 0).
Row 2: P0 (1: 0: 0: 1), K2 (3: 0: 2: 3), ★P3, K3, rep from ★ to last 5 (1: 3: 5: 1) sts, P3 (1: 3: 3: 1), K2 (0: 0: 2: 0).
These 2 rows form rib.

Work in rib for a further 15 rows, ending with a RS row.
Row 18 (WS): Rib 19 (21: 23: 25: 27), (M1, rib 1) 4 times, M1, rib 8, (M1, rib 1) 5 times, M1, rib 5, (M1, rib 1) 3 times, M1, rib 5, (M1, rib 1) 3 times, (rib 1, M1) 3 times, rib 5, (M1, rib 1) 3 times, M1, rib 5, (M1, rib 1) 5 times, M1, rib 8, (M1, rib 1) 4 times, M1, rib to last st, inc in last st. 140 (144: 148: 152: 156) sts.
Change to 5mm (US 8) needles.
Starting and ending rows as indicated and repeating the 28 row pattern repeat throughout, cont in patt from chart for back until back measures 45 (45: 46: 46: 47) cm, ending with a WS row.
Shape armholes
Keeping patt correct, cast off 5 sts at beg of next 2 rows. 130 (134: 138: 142: 146) sts.
Dec 1 st at each end of next 5 rows. 120 (124: 128: 132: 136) sts.
Cont straight until armhole measures 22 (23: 23: 24: 24) cm, ending with a WS row.
Shape shoulders and back neck
Cast off 13 (14: 14: 15: 15) sts at beg of next 2 rows. 94 (96: 100: 102: 106) sts.
Next row (RS): Cast off 13 (14: 14: 15: 15) sts, patt until there are 18 (17: 19: 18: 19) sts on right needle and turn, leaving rem sts on a holder.
Work each side of neck separately.
Cast off 4 sts at beg of next row.
Cast off rem 14 (13: 15: 14: 15) sts.
With RS facing, rejoin yarn to rem sts, cast off centre 32 (34: 34: 36: 38) sts decreasing 14 sts evenly, patt to end.
Complete to match first side, reversing shapings.

FRONT

Work as given for back until 12 (12: 14: 14: 14) rows less have been worked than on back to start of shoulder shaping, ending with a WS row.
Shape neck
Next row (RS): Patt 49 (50: 53: 54: 55) sts and turn, leaving rem sts on a holder.
Work each side of neck separately.
Cast off 4 sts at beg of next row.
45 (46: 49: 50: 51) sts.
Dec 1 st at neck edge of next 3 rows, then on foll 1 (1: 2: 2: 2) alt rows, then on foll 4th row.
40 (41: 43: 44: 45) sts.
Work 1 row, ending with a WS row.
Shape shoulder
Cast off 13 (14: 14: 15: 15) sts at beg of next and foll alt row.
Work 1 row.
Cast off rem 14 (13: 15: 14: 15) sts.
With RS facing, rejoin yarn to rem sts, cast off centre 22 (24: 22: 24: 26) sts decreasing 10 (12: 10: 12: 12) sts evenly, patt to end.
Complete to match first side, reversing shapings.

SLEEVES (both alike)

Cast on 43 (43: 45: 47: 47) sts using 4mm (US 6) needles.
Row 1 (RS): K2 (2: 0: 0: 0), P3 (3: 0: 1: 1), ★K3, P3, rep from ★ to last 2 (2: 3: 4: 4) sts, K2 (2: 3: 3: 3), P0 (0: 0: 1: 1).
Row 2: P2 (2: 0: 0: 0), K3 (3: 0: 1: 1), ★P3, K3, rep from ★ to last 2 (2: 3: 4: 4) sts, P2 (2: 3: 3: 3), K0 (0: 0: 1: 1).
These 2 rows form rib.
Work in rib for a further 15 rows, ending with a RS row.
Row 18 (WS): Rib 14 (14: 15: 16: 16), (M1, rib 1) 5 times, M1, rib 5, (M1, rib 1) 5 times,

M1, rib to end.
55 (55: 57: 59: 59) sts.
Change to 5mm (US 8) needles.
Starting and ending rows as indicated and repeating the 14 row pattern repeat throughout, cont in patt from chart for sleeves, shaping sides

28 row patt rep

C12B
C12F

C11B

Cr8R
Cr8L

Cr4R
Cr4L
C6B

Key
□ K on RS, P on WS
■ P on RS, K on WS
⊡ K1 tbl on RS, P1 tbl on WS

Back chart

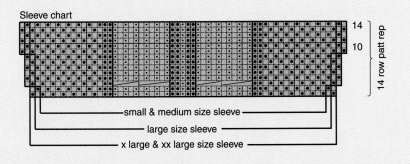

Sleeve chart

14
10

14 row patt rep

small & medium size sleeve
large size sleeve
x large & xx large size sleeve

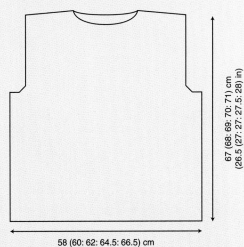

67 (68: 69: 70: 71) cm
(26.5 (27: 27: 27.5: 28) in)

58 (60: 62: 64.5: 66.5) cm
(23 (23.5: 24.5: 25.5: 26) in)

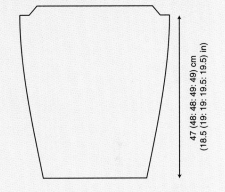

47 (48: 48: 49: 49) cm
(18.5 (19: 19: 19.5: 19.5) in)

by inc 1 st at each end of 3rd and every foll 6th row to 67 (63: 69: 69: 69) sts, then on every foll 4th row until there are 89 (93: 93: 97: 97) sts, taking inc sts into patt.

Cont straight until sleeve measures 47 (48: 48: 49: 49) cm, ending with a WS row.

Shape top
Keeping patt correct, cast off 5 sts at beg of next 2 rows. 79 (83: 83: 87: 87) sts.
Dec 1 st at each end of next and foll 4 alt rows, then on foll row, ending with a WS row.
Cast off rem 67 (71: 71: 75: 75) sts.

MAKING UP
PRESS as described on the information page.
Join right shoulder seam using back stitch, or mattress st if preferred.

Collar
With RS facing and using 4mm (US 6) needles, pick up and knit 16 (17: 18: 19: 18) sts down left side of neck, 10 (12: 10: 12: 14) sts from front, 16 (17: 18: 19: 18) sts up right side of neck, then 27 (29: 29: 31: 31) sts from back.
69 (75: 75: 81: 81) sts.
Row 1 (WS): P3, *K3, P3, rep from * to end.
Row 2: K3, *P3, K3, rep from * to end.
These 2 rows form rib.
Cont in rib until collar measures 5 cm.
Change to 5mm (US 8) needles.
Cont in rib until collar measures 16 cm.
Cast off in rib.
See information page for finishing instructions, setting in sleeves using the shallow set-in method and reversing collar seam for turn-back.

Design number 4

WILLOW

KIM HARGREAVES

YARN

	XS	S	M	L	XL	
To fit bust	81	86	91	97	102	cm
	32	34	36	38	40	in
Rowan Yorkshire Tweed Chunky						
A String	551 11	11	11	12	12	13 x100gm
B Stout	554 1	1	1	1	1	x100gm

NEEDLES
1 pair 7mm (no 2) (US 10½) needles
1 pair 8mm (no 0) (US 11) needles
Cable needle

BUTTONS - 5 x 75340

TENSION
12 sts and 16 rows to 10 cm measured over stocking stitch using 8mm (US 11) needles.

SPECIAL ABBREVIATIONS
C6B = Cable 6 back Slip next 3 sts onto cable needle and leave at back of work, K3, then K3 from cable needle
C6F = Cable 6 front Slip next 3 sts onto cable needle and leave at front of work, K3, then K3 from cable needle

BACK
Cast on 76 (80: 82: 86: 88) sts using 7mm (US 10½) needles and yarn A.
Row 1 (RS): K1 (0: 0: 0: 0), P2 (1: 2: 0: 1), *K2, P2, rep from * to last 1 (3: 0: 2: 3) sts, K1 (2: 0: 2: 2), P0 (1: 0: 0: 1).
Row 2: P1 (0: 0: 0: 0), K2 (1: 2: 0: 1), *P2, K2, rep from * to last 1 (3: 0: 2: 3) sts, P1 (2: 0: 2: 2), K0 (1: 0: 0: 1).
These 2 rows form rib.
Work in rib for a further 12 rows, ending with a WS row.
Change to 8mm (US 11) needles.
Row 1 (RS): K9 (11: 12: 14: 15), (P2, C6F, P2, K6) twice, P2, C6B, P2, K6, P2, C6B, P2, K to end.
Row 2 and every foll alt row: P9 (11: 12: 14: 15), (K2, P6) 7 times, K2, P to end.

Rows 3, 5 and 7: K9 (11: 12: 14: 15), (P2, K6) 7 times, P2, K to end.
Row 8: As row 2.
These 8 rows form cable patt.
Cont in patt until back measures 56 (57: 57: 58: 58) cm, ending with a WS row.
Shape armholes
Keeping patt correct, cast off 3 (4: 4: 5: 5) sts at beg of next 2 rows. 70 (72: 74: 76: 78) sts.
Dec 1 st at each end of next 3 rows, then on foll 2 (2: 3: 3: 4) alt rows. 60 (62: 62: 64: 64) sts.
Cont straight until armhole measures 23 (23: 24: 24: 25) cm, ending with a WS row.
Shape shoulders and back neck
Cast off 6 (7: 7: 7: 7) sts at beg of next 2 rows. 48 (48: 48: 50: 50) sts.
Next row (RS): Cast off 6 (7: 7: 7: 7) sts, patt until there are 10 (9: 9: 9: 9) sts on right needle and turn, leaving rem sts on a holder.
Work each side of neck separately.
Cast off 3 sts at beg of next row.
Cast off rem 7 (6: 6: 6: 6) sts.
With RS facing, rejoin yarn to rem sts, cast off centre 16 (16: 16: 18: 18) sts, patt to end.
Complete to match first side, reversing shapings.

POCKET LININGS (make 2)
Cast on 16 sts using 8mm (US 11) needles and yarn A.
Beg with a K row, work in st st for 24 rows, inc 1 st at each end of last row. 18 sts.
Break yarn and leave sts on a holder.

LEFT FRONT
Cast on 39 (41: 42: 44: 45) sts using 7mm (US 10½) needles and yarn A.

Row 1 (RS): K1 (0: 0: 0: 0), P2 (1: 2: 0: 1), ★K2, P2, rep from ★ to end.
Row 2: K2, ★P2, K2, rep from ★ to last 1 (3: 0: 2: 3) sts, P1 (2: 0: 2: 2), K0 (1: 0: 0: 1).
These 2 rows form rib.
Work in rib for a further 12 rows, ending with a WS row.
Change to 8mm (US 11) needles.
Row 1 (RS): K9 (11: 12: 14: 15), P2, C6F, P2, K6, P2, C6F, P2, K4.
Row 2 and every foll alt row: P4, (K2, P6) 3 times, K2, P to end.
Rows 3, 5 and 7: K9 (11: 12: 14: 15), (P2, K6) 3 times, P2, K4.
Row 8: As row 2.
These 8 rows form cable patt.
Work in patt for a further 12 rows, ending with a WS row.
Place pocket
Next row (RS): K5 (7: 8: 10: 11), slip next 18 sts onto a holder and, in their place, patt across 18 sts of first pocket lining, patt to end.
Cont straight until left front matches back to beg of armhole shaping, ending with a WS row.
Shape armhole
Keeping patt correct, cast off 3 (4: 4: 5: 5) sts at beg of next row. 36 (37: 38: 39: 40) sts.
Work 1 row.
Dec 1 st at armhole edge of next 3 rows, then on foll 2 (2: 3: 3: 4) alt rows. 31 (32: 32: 33: 33) sts.
Cont straight until 13 (13: 13: 15: 15) rows less have been worked than on back to start of shoulder shaping, ending with a RS row.
Shape neck
Next row (WS): Patt 6 sts and slip these sts onto a holder, patt to end. 25 (26: 26: 27: 27) sts.
Dec 1 st at neck edge of next 4 rows, then on foll 2 (2: 2: 3: 3) alt rows. 19 (20: 20: 20: 20) sts.
Work 4 rows, ending with a WS row.
Shape shoulder
Cast off 6 (7: 7: 7: 7) sts at beg of next and foll alt row.
Work 1 row.
Cast off rem 7 (6: 6: 6: 6) sts.

RIGHT FRONT
Cast on 39 (41: 42: 44: 45) sts using 7mm (US 10½) needles and yarn A.
Row 1 (RS): P2, ★K2, P2, rep from ★ to last 1 (3: 0: 2: 3) sts, K1 (2: 0: 2: 2), P0 (1: 0: 0: 1).
Row 2: P1 (0: 0: 0: 0), K2 (1: 2: 0: 1), ★P2, K2, rep from ★ to end.
These 2 rows form rib.
Work in rib for a further 12 rows, ending with a WS row.
Change to 8mm (US 11) needles.
Row 1 (RS): K4, P2, C6B, P2, K6, P2, C6B, P2, K to end.
Row 2 and every foll alt row: P9 (11: 12: 14: 15), (K2, P6) 3 times, K2, P4.
Rows 3, 5 and 7: K4, (P2, K6) 3 times, P2, K to end.
Row 8: As row 2.
These 8 rows form cable patt.
Work in patt for a further 12 rows, ending with a WS row.
Place pocket
Next row (RS): Patt 16 sts, slip next 18 sts onto a holder and, in their place, patt across 18 sts of second pocket lining, patt to end.
Complete to match left front, reversing shapings.

SLEEVES (both alike)
Cast on 40 (42: 42: 44: 44) sts using 7mm (US 10½) needles and yarn B.

Row 1 (RS): K0 (0: 0: 1: 1), P1 (2: 2: 2: 2), ★K2, P2, rep from ★ to last 3 (0: 0: 1: 1) sts, K2 (0: 0: 1: 1), P1 (0: 0: 0: 0).
Break off yarn B and join in yarn A.
Row 2: P0 (0: 0: 1: 1), K1 (2: 2: 2: 2), ★P2, K2, rep from ★ to last 3 (0: 0: 1: 1) sts, P2 (0: 0: 1: 1), K1 (0: 0: 0: 0).
These 2 rows form rib.
Work in rib for a further 12 rows, ending with a WS row.
Change to 8mm (US 11) needles.
Row 1 (RS): Inc in first st, K6 (7: 7: 8: 8), P2, C6F, P2, K6, P2, C6B, P2, K to last st, inc in last st. 42 (44: 44: 46: 46) sts.
Row 2 and every foll alt row: P8 (9: 9: 10: 10), (K2, P6) 3 times, K2, P to end.
Rows 3, 5 and 7: K8 (9: 9: 10: 10), (P2, K6) 3 times, P2, K to end.
Row 8: As row 2.
These 8 rows form cable patt.
Cont in patt, shaping sides by inc 1 st at each end of 9th (9th: 5th: 5th: 3rd) and every foll 14th (14th: 12th: 12th: 10th) row to 48 (50: 50: 52: 52) sts, then on every foll – (–: 10th: 10th: 8th) row until there are – (–: 52: 54: 56) sts.
Cont straight until sleeve measures 41 (41: 42: 42: 42) cm, ending with a WS row.
Shape top
Keeping patt correct, cast off 3 (4: 4: 5: 5) sts at beg of next 2 rows. 42 (42: 44: 44: 46) sts.
Dec 1 st at each end of next and foll alt row, then on every foll 4th row until 32 (32: 34: 34: 36) sts rem.
Work 1 row.
Dec 1 st at each end of next and every foll alt row until 28 sts rem, then on foll row, ending with a WS row.
Cast off 4 sts at beg of next 2 rows.
Cast off rem 18 sts.

MAKING UP
PRESS as described on the information page.
Join both shoulder seams using back stitch.
Button band
Cast on 4 sts using 7mm (US 10½) needles and yarn A.
Row 1 (RS): (K1, P1) twice.
Row 2: (P1, K1) twice.
These 2 rows form moss st.
Cont in moss st until band, when slightly stretched, fits up left front opening edge to neck shaping, ending with a WS row.
Break yarn and leave sts on a holder.
Slip stitch band in place.
Mark positions for 5 buttons on this band – first to come 17 cm up from cast-on edge, last to come just below neck shaping, and rem 3 buttons evenly spaced between.
Buttonhole band
Work as given for button band, with the addition of 5 buttonholes worked to correspond with positions marked for buttons as folls:
Buttonhole row (RS): K1, P2tog, yrn, P1.
Do NOT break yarn.
Slip stitch band in place.
Collar
With RS facing, using 7mm (US 10½) needles and yarn A, moss st 4 sts of buttonhole band, work across 6 sts from right front holder as folls: P2, K2, P2, pick up and knit 21 (21: 21: 23: 23) sts up right side of neck, 28 (28: 28: 32: 32) sts from back, and 21 (21: 21: 23: 23) sts down left side of neck, work across 6 sts from left front holder as folls: P2, K2, P2, then moss st 4 sts of button band. 90 (90: 90: 98: 98) sts.

Row 1 (WS of body, RS of collar): Moss st 4 sts, K2, ★P2, K2, rep from ★ to last 4 sts, moss st 4 sts.
Row 2: Moss st 4 sts, P2, ★K2, P2, rep from ★ to last 4 sts, moss st 4 sts.
These 2 rows set the sts – first and last 4 sts in moss st with rib between.
Cont as set until collar measures 17 cm, ending with row 2.
Join in yarn B.
Using yarn B, work 2 rows.
Using yarn A, work 2 rows.
Rep last 4 rows twice more.
Using yarn A, cast off in patt.
Pocket borders (both alike)
With RS facing and using 7mm (US 10½) needles, rejoin yarn A to 18 sts from pocket holder and cont as folls:
Row 1 (RS): (P2, K2) 4 times, P2.
Row 2: K2, (P2, K2) 4 times.
Rep last 2 rows once more.
Cast off in rib.
Belt
Cast on 1 st using 7mm (US 10½) needles and yarn A.
Row 1 (RS): K1.
Row 2: P into front, K into back, then P into front of st. 3 sts.
Row 3: P1, K1, P1.
Row 4: K into front then P into back of first st, K1, P into front then K into back of last st. 5 sts.
Row 5: K1, (P1, K1) twice.
Rep last row until belt measures 130 cm.
Next row: P2tog, K1, P2tog.
Next row: P1, K1, P1.
Next row: Sl 1, K2tog, psso and fasten off.
See information page for finishing instructions, setting in sleeves using the set-in method. Make two 22 cm long tassels using yarn A and attach to ends of belt.

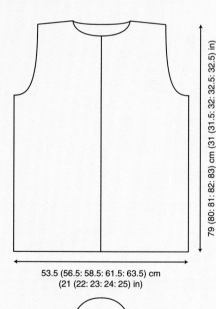

79 (80: 81: 82: 83) cm (31 (31.5: 32: 32.5: 32.5) in)

53.5 (56.5: 58.5: 61.5: 63.5) cm (21 (22: 23: 24: 25) in)

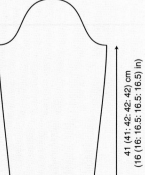

41 (41: 42: 42: 42) cm (16 (16: 16.5: 16.5: 16.5) in)

Design number 5

WISPY

KIM HARGREAVES

YARN
To fit average size adult foot
Rowan Yorkshire Tweed 4 ply
Multi coloured socks

A Butterscotch	272	1	x	25gm
B Graze	286	1	x	25gm
C Deep Aubergine	280	1	x	25gm
D Radiant	276	1	x	25gm
E Foxy	275	1	x	25gm
F Glory	273	1	x	25gm
G Bristle	278	1	x	25gm
H Knight	281	1	x	25gm
J Oceanic	285	1	x	25gm
L Cheerful	271	1	x	25gm

Three colour socks

A Radiant	276	2	x	25gm
B Butterscotch	272	2	x	25gm
C Explode	277	1	x	25gm

NEEDLES
1 pair 2¼mm (no 13) (US 1) needles
1 pair 3mm (no 11) (US 2/3) needles

TENSION
28 sts and 40 rows to 10 cm measured over
stocking stitch using 3mm (US 2/3) needles.

MULTI COLOURED SOCKS (make 2 alike)
Cast on 58 sts using 2¼mm (US 1) needles and
yarn B.
Break off yarn B and join in yarn A.
Row 1 (RS): K2, *P2, K2, rep from * to end.
Row 2: P2, *K2, P2, rep from * to end.
These 2 rows form rib.
Work in rib for a further 10 rows, inc 1 st at end
of last row and ending with a WS row.
59 sts.
Change to 3mm (US 2/3) needles.★★★
Beg with a K row, cont in st st as folls:
Rows 13 and 14: Using yarn D.
Rows 15 and 16: Using yarn C.
Rows 17 to 20: Using yarn H.
Rows 21 and 22: Using yarn L.
Rows 23 and 24: Using yarn B.
Rows 25 and 26: Using yarn J.
Rows 27 and 28: Using yarn E.

Rows 29 and 30: Using yarn G.
Rows 31 to 34: Using yarn F.
Rows 35 and 36: Using yarn A.
Row 37: Using yarn D.
Row 38: Using yarn G.
Rows 39 and 40: Using yarn E.
Rows 41 and 42: Using yarn C.
Rows 43 to 46: Using yarn D.
Row 47: Using yarn J.
Rows 48 and 49: Using yarn L.
Rows 50 to 53: Using yarn B, dec 1 st at each
end of last of these rows. 57 sts.
Row 54: Using yarn A.
Rows 55 and 56: Using yarn F.
Rows 57 and 58: Using yarn G.
Rows 59 to 61: Using yarn E.
Rows 62 and 63: Using yarn J.
Row 64: Using yarn B.
Row 65: Using yarn A.
Rows 66 and 67: Using yarn L.
Rows 68 and 69: Using yarn H.
Rows 70 to 72: Using yarn C.
Rows 73 to 76: Using yarn D, dec 1 st at each
end of first of these rows.
55 sts.
Row 77: Using yarn E.
Row 78: Using yarn G.
Rows 79 and 80: Using yarn F.
Rows 81 and 82: Using yarn C.
Rows 83 and 84: Using yarn G.
Rows 85 and 86: Using yarn F.
Rows 87 to 89: Using yarn A.
Rows 90 and 91: Using yarn B.
Rows 92 to 94: Using yarn L.
Rows 95 and 96: Using yarn J.
Row 97: Using yarn H.
Rows 98 to 100: Using yarn C.
Shape heel
★★Using yarn C only, cont as folls:
Row 101 (RS): K15 and turn.
Row 102 and every foll alt row: Purl.
Row 103: K14 and turn.
Row 105: K13 and turn.
Row 107: K12 and turn.
Cont in this way until "K7 and turn" has been
worked.
Row 118: Purl.
Row 119: K8 and turn.
Row 121: K9 and turn.
Row 123: K10 and turn.
Cont in this way until "K15 and turn" as been
worked.
Row 134: P15.
Break yarn.★★
Slip all 55 sts onto other needle and rejoin yarn
C with **WS** facing.
Reading K for P and P for K, rep from ★★ to ★★
once more.
Shape foot
Slip all 55 sts onto other needle and rejoin yarn
E with RS facing.
Cont in stripes over all sts as folls:
Rows 135 and 136: Using yarn E.
Rows 137 and 138: Using yarn D.
Row 139: Using yarn C.
Row 140: Using yarn L.
Rows 141 to 143: Using yarn A.
Row 144: Using yarn B.
Row 145: Using yarn L.
Row 146: Using yarn A.
Rows 147 to 149: Using yarn B.
Rows 150 and 151: Using yarn J.
Rows 152 and 153: Using yarn L.
Row 154: Using yarn D.
Row 155: Using yarn C.

Row 156: Using yarn F.
Rows 157 and 158: Using yarn G.
Rows 159 to 161: Using yarn E.
Row 162: Using yarn J.
Rows 163 to 165: Using yarn H.
Rows 166 and 167: Using yarn L.
Row 168: Using yarn B.
Row 169: Using yarn A.
Row 170: Using yarn F.
Row 171: Using yarn G.
Row 172: Using yarn D.
Rows 173 and 174: Using yarn J.
Rows 175 to 177: Using yarn F.
Rows 178 and 179: Using yarn E.
Rows 180 and 181: Using yarn G.
Rows 182 to 185: Using yarn C.
Rows 186 and 187: Using yarn H.
Rows 188 and 189: Using yarn J.
Row 190: Using yarn C.
Shape toe
Using yarn C only, cont as folls:
Row 191 (RS): K11, K2tog, K2, K2tog tbl,
K21, K2tog, K2, K2tog tbl, K11.
Row 192 and every foll alt row: Purl.
Row 193: K10, K2tog, K2, K2tog tbl, K19,
K2tog, K2, K2tog tbl, K10.
Row 195: K9, K2tog, K2, K2tog tbl, K17,
K2tog, K2, K2tog tbl, K9.
Row 197: K8, K2tog, K2, K2tog tbl, K15,
K2tog, K2, K2tog tbl, K8.
Row 199: K7, K2tog, K2, K2tog tbl, K13,
K2tog, K2, K2tog tbl, K7.
Row 201: K6, K2tog, K2, K2tog tbl, K11,
K2tog, K2, K2tog tbl, K6.
Row 203: K5, K2tog, K2, K2tog tbl, K9, K2tog,
K2, K2tog tbl, K5.
Row 205: K4, K2tog, K2, K2tog tbl, K7, K2tog,
K2, K2tog tbl, K4.
Row 207: K3, K2tog, K2, K2tog tbl, K5, K2tog,
K2, K2tog tbl, K3. 19 sts.
Row 208: Purl.
Cast off.

MAKING UP
PRESS as described on the information page.
Join back and toe seam using back stitch, or a
flat seam if preferred.

THREE COLOUR SOCKS (make 2 alike)
Work as given for multi coloured socks to ★★★.
Beg with a K row, cont in st st as folls:
Rows 13 and 14: Using yarn A.
Rows 15 and 16: Using yarn B.
These 4 rows form striped st st.
Work a further 84 rows in striped st st, dec 1 st
at each end of rows 53 and 73 and ending after
2 rows using yarn B.
55 sts.
Shape heel
Using yarn C only, work as given for multi
coloured socks.
Shape foot
Slip all 55 sts onto other needle and rejoin yarn
A with RS facing.
Beg with 2 rows using yarn A, cont in striped st
st as before over all sts as folls:
Work 56 rows, ending with a WS row.
Shape toe
Using yarn C only, work as given for multi
coloured socks.

MAKING UP
PRESS as described on the information page.
Join back and toe seam using back stitch, or a
flat seam if preferred.

OAKWORTH

SARAH DALLAS

YARN

	XS	S	M	L	XL	
To fit bust	81	86	91	97	102	cm
	32	34	36	38	40	in

Rowan Yorkshire Tweed 4 ply
Sweater

A Enchant	268	7	8	8	9	9 x 25gm
B Mulled Wine	279	2	2	2	2	2 x 25gm
C Foxy	275	1	1	1	1	1 x 25gm
D Butterscotch	272	1	1	1	1	1 x 25gm

Cardigan

A Enchant	268	10	10	11	11	12 x 25gm
B Mulled Wine	279	3	3	3	4	4 x 25gm
C Foxy	275	1	1	1	1	1 x 25gm
D Butterscotch	272	1	1	1	1	1 x 25gm

NEEDLES

1 pair 2¾mm (no 12) (US 2) needles
1 pair 3¼mm (no 10) (US 3) needles

BUTTONS – 9 x 75320 for cardigan

TENSION

28 sts and 38 rows to 10 cm measured over patterned stocking stitch using 3¼mm (US 3) needles.

Sweater

BACK

Cast on 109 (115: 123: 129: 137) sts using 2¾mm (US 2) needles and yarn D.
Break off yarn D and join in yarn A.
Row 1 (RS): K1, *P1, K1, rep from * to end.
Row 2: P1, *K1, P1, rep from * to end.
These 2 rows form rib.
Cont in rib until back measures 6.5 cm, ending with a WS row.
Change to 3¼mm (US 3) needles.
Using the **fairisle** technique as described on the information page, starting and ending rows as indicated, working rows 1 to 12 once only and then **repeating chart rows 13 to 20 throughout**, cont in patt from chart for sweater, which is worked entirely in st st beg with a K row, as folls:
Inc 1 st at each end of 3rd and every foll 12th row until there are 121 (127: 135: 141: 149) sts, taking inc sts into patt.
Cont straight until back measures 28 (29: 29: 30: 30) cm, ending with a WS row.
Shape armholes
Keeping patt correct, cast off 6 (7: 7: 8: 8) sts at beg of next 2 rows. 109 (113: 121: 125: 133) sts.
Dec 1 st at each end of next 5 (5: 7: 7: 9) rows, then on foll 1 (2: 2: 3: 3) alt rows, then on every foll 4th row until 93 (95: 99: 101: 105) sts rem.
Cont straight until armhole measures 20 (20: 21: 21: 22) cm, ending with a WS row.
Shape shoulders and back neck
Cast off 8 (8: 9: 9: 9) sts at beg of next 2 rows. 77 (79: 81: 83: 87) sts.
Next row (RS): Cast off 8 (8: 9: 9: 9) sts, patt until there are 12 (12: 12: 12: 14) sts on right needle and turn, leaving rem sts on a holder.
Work each side of neck separately.
Cast off 4 sts at beg of next row.
Cast off rem 8 (8: 8: 8: 10) sts.
With RS facing, rejoin yarns to rem sts, cast off centre 37 (39: 39: 41: 41) sts, patt to end.
Complete to match first side, reversing shapings.

FRONT

Work as given for back until 20 (20: 20: 22: 22) rows less have been worked than on back to start of shoulder shaping, ending with a WS row.
Shape neck
Next row (RS): Patt 37 (37: 39: 40: 42) sts and turn, leaving rem sts on a holder.
Work each side of neck separately.
Cast off 4 sts at beg of next row.
33 (33: 35: 36: 38) sts.
Dec 1 st at neck edge of next 5 rows, then on foll 3 (3: 3: 4: 4) alt rows, then on foll 4th row.
24 (24: 26: 26: 28) sts.
Work 3 rows, ending with a WS row.
Shape shoulder
Cast off 8 (8: 9: 9: 9) sts at beg of next and foll alt row.
Work 1 row.
Cast off rem 8 (8: 8: 8: 10) sts.
With RS facing, rejoin yarns to rem sts, cast off centre 19 (21: 21: 21: 21) sts, patt to end.
Complete to match first side, reversing shapings.

SLEEVES (both alike)

Cast on 81 (83: 87: 89: 93) sts using 2¾mm (US 2) needles and yarn D.
Break off yarn D and join in yarn A.
Work in rib as given for back for 16 rows, inc 1 st at each end of 11th and foll 4th of these rows and ending with a WS row. 85 (87: 91: 93: 97) sts.
Change to 3¼mm (US 3) needles.
Starting and ending rows as indicated, working rows 1 to 12 once only and then **repeating chart rows 13 to 20 throughout**, cont in patt from chart for sweater as folls:
Inc 1 st at each end of 3rd and every foll 4th row until there are 95 (97: 101: 103: 107) sts, taking inc sts into patt.
Cont straight until sleeve measures 11 cm, ending with a WS row.
Shape top
Keeping patt correct, cast off 6 (7: 7: 8: 8) sts at beg of next 2 rows. 83 (83: 87: 87: 91) sts.
Dec 1 st at each end of next 5 rows, then on foll 3 alt rows, then on every foll 4th row until 61 (61: 65: 65: 69) sts rem.
Work 1 row, ending with a WS row.
Dec 1 st at each end of next and every foll alt row to 53 sts, then on foll 3 rows, ending with a WS row. 47 sts.
Cast off 5 sts at beg of next 6 rows.
Cast off rem 17 sts.

MAKING UP

PRESS as described on the information page.
Join right shoulder seam using back stitch, or mattress st if preferred.
Neckband
With RS facing, using 2¾mm (US 2) needles and yarn A, pick up and knit 24 (24: 24: 26: 26) sts down left side of neck, 19 (21: 21: 21: 21) sts from front, 24 (24: 24: 26: 26) sts up right side of neck, then 46 (48: 48: 50: 50) sts from back. 113 (117: 117: 123: 123) sts.
Work in rib as given for back for 2 cm.
Cast off in rib.
See information page for finishing instructions, setting in sleeves using the set-in method.

Cardigan

BACK

Cast on 117 (123: 131: 137: 145) sts using 2¾mm (US 2) needles and yarn D.
Break off yarn D and join in yarn A.
Row 1 (RS): K1, *P1, K1, rep from * to end.
Row 2: P1, *K1, P1, rep from * to end.
These 2 rows form rib.
Cont in rib until back measures 6.5 cm, ending with a WS row.
Change to 3¼mm (US 3) needles.
Using the **fairisle** technique as described on the information page, starting and ending rows as indicated and **repeating chart rows 1 to 8 only**, cont in patt from chart for cardigan, which is worked entirely in st st beg with a K row, as folls:
Inc 1 st at each end of 3rd and every foll 12th row until there are 129 (135: 143: 149: 157) sts, taking inc sts into patt.
Cont straight until back measures approx 28 (29: 29: 30: 30) cm, ending after chart row 6 and with a WS row.
Shape armholes
Keeping patt correct, cast off 7 (8: 8: 9: 9) sts at beg of next 2 rows, ending with chart row 8. 115 (119: 127: 131: 139) sts.
Now working chart rows 9 to 62 **once only** and then completing work by repeating rows 63 to 70 **only**, cont as folls:
Dec 1 st at each end of next 5 (5: 7: 7: 9) rows, then on foll 2 (3: 3: 4: 4) alt rows, then on every foll 4th row until 97 (99: 103: 105: 109) sts rem.
Cont straight until armhole measures 21 (21: 22: 22: 23) cm, ending with a WS row.

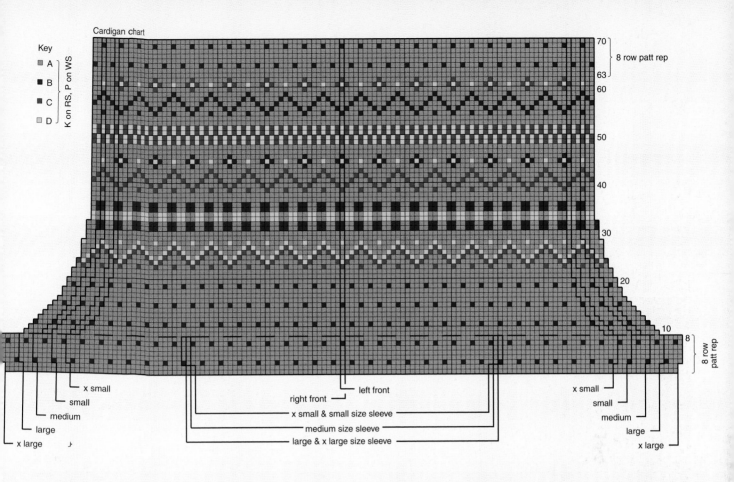

Cardigan chart

Key
- A
- B
- C
- D

K on RS, P on WS

8 row patt rep

x small
small
medium
large
x large

right front — left front

x small & small size sleeve
medium size sleeve
large & x large size sleeve

x small
small
medium
large
x large

8 row patt rep

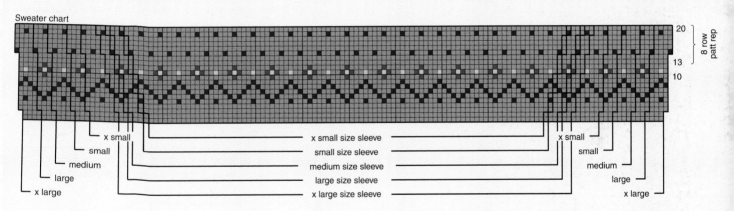

Sweater chart

8 row patt rep

x small
small
medium
large
x large

x small size sleeve
small size sleeve
medium size sleeve
large size sleeve
x large size sleeve

x small
small
medium
large
x large

Shape shoulders and back neck

Cast off 9 (9: 9: 9: 10) sts at beg of next 2 rows.
79 (81: 85: 87: 89) sts.

Next row (RS): Cast off 9 (9: 9: 9: 10) sts, patt until there are 12 (12: 14: 14: 14) sts on right needle and turn, leaving rem sts on a holder.
Work each side of neck separately.
Cast off 4 sts at beg of next row.
Cast off rem 8 (8: 10: 10: 10) sts.
With RS facing, rejoin yarns to rem sts, cast off centre 37 (39: 39: 41: 41) sts, patt to end.
Complete to match first side, reversing shapings.

LEFT FRONT

Cast on 65 (67: 71: 75: 79) sts using 2¾mm
(US 2) needles and yarn D.
Break off yarn D and join in yarn A.
Work in rib as given for back for 6.5 cm, ending with a RS row.

Next row (WS): Rib 7 and slip these sts onto a holder, M1, rib to last 0 (1: 1: 0: 0) st, (inc in last st) 0 (1: 1: 0: 0) times. 59 (62: 66: 69: 73) sts.

Change to 3¼mm (US 3) needles.
Starting and ending rows as indicated and **repeating chart rows 1 to 8 only**, cont in patt from chart for cardigan as folls:
Inc 1 st at beg of 3rd and every foll 12th row until there are 65 (68: 72: 75: 79) sts, taking inc sts into patt.
Cont straight until left front matches back to beg of armhole shaping, ending after chart row 6 and with a WS row.

Shape armholes

Keeping patt correct, cast off 7 (8: 8: 9: 9) sts at beg of next row. 58 (60: 64: 66: 70) sts.
Work 1 row, ending with chart row 8.
Now working chart rows 9 to 62 **once only** and then completing work by repeating rows 63 to 70 **only**, cont as folls:
Dec 1 st at armhole edge of next 5 (5: 7: 7: 9) rows, then on foll 2 (3: 3: 4: 4) alt rows, then on every foll 4th row until 49 (50: 52: 53: 55) sts rem.
Cont straight until 21 (21: 21: 23: 23) rows less have been worked than on back to start of shoulder shaping, ending with a RS row.

Shape neck

Keeping patt correct, cast off 8 (9: 9: 9: 9) sts at beg of next row, then 6 sts at beg of foll alt row.
35 (35: 37: 38: 40) sts.
Dec 1 st at neck edge of next 5 rows, then on foll 3 (3: 3: 4: 4) alt rows, then on foll 4th row.
26 (26: 28: 28: 30) sts.
Work 3 rows, ending with a WS row.

Shape shoulder

Cast off 9 (9: 9: 9: 10) sts at beg of next and foll alt row.
Work 1 row.
Cast off rem 8 (8: 10: 10: 10) sts.

RIGHT FRONT

Cast on 65 (67: 71: 75: 79) sts using 2¾mm
(US 2) needles and yarn D.
Break off yarn D and join in yarn A.
Work in rib as given for back for 4 rows, ending with a WS row.

Row 5 (buttonhole row) (RS): K1, P1, K2tog, yfwd, rib to end.

Cont in rib until right front measures 5.5 cm, ending with a WS row.
Next row (RS): As row 5.
Cont in rib until right front measures 6.5 cm, ending with a RS row.
Next row (WS): (Inc in first st) 0 (1: 1: 0: 0) times, rib to last 7 sts, M1 and turn, leaving last 7 sts on a holder. 59 (62: 66: 69: 73) sts.
Change to 3¼mm (US 3) needles.
Starting and ending rows as indicated and **repeating chart rows 1 to 8 only**, cont in patt from chart for cardigan as folls:
Inc 1 st at end of 3rd and every foll 12th row until there are 65 (68: 72: 75: 79) sts, taking inc sts into patt.
Complete to match left front, reversing shapings.

SLEEVES (both alike)
Cast on 63 (63: 65: 67: 67) sts using 2¾mm (US 2) needles and yarn D.
Break off yarn D and join in yarn A.
Work in rib as given for back for 5 cm, ending with a WS row.
Change to 3¼mm (US 3) needles.
Starting and ending rows as indicated and **repeating chart rows 1 to 8 only**, cont in patt from chart for cardigan as folls:
Inc 1 st at each end of 3rd and every foll 10th (8th: 8th: 8th: 8th) row to 69 (95: 93: 95: 83) sts, then on every foll 8th (6th: 6th: 6th: 6th) row until there are 97 (99: 103: 105: 109) sts, taking inc sts into patt.
Cont straight until sleeve measures approx 44 (44: 45: 45: 45) cm, ending after chart row 6 and with a WS row.
Now working chart rows 9 to 62 **once only** and then completing work by repeating rows 63 to 70 **only**, cont as folls:
Work 4 rows, ending with chart row 12.
Shape top
Keeping patt correct, cast off 7 (8: 8: 9: 9) sts at beg of next 2 rows. 83 (83: 87: 87: 91) sts.
Dec 1 st at each end of next 5 rows, then on foll 3 alt rows, then on every foll 4th row until 59 (59: 63: 63: 67) sts rem.
Work 1 row, ending with a WS row.
Dec 1 st at each end of next and every foll alt row to 49 sts, then on foll 5 rows, ending with a WS row. 39 sts.
Cast off 5 sts at beg of next 4 rows.
Cast off rem 19 sts.

MAKING UP
PRESS as described on the information page.
Join both shoulder seams using back stitch, or mattress st if preferred.
Button band
Slip 7 sts from left front holder onto 2¾mm (US 2) needles and rejoin yarn A with RS facing.
Cont in rib as set until band, when slightly stretched, fits up left front opening edge to neck shaping, ending with a WS row.
Break yarn and leave sts on a holder.
Slip stitch band in place.
Mark positions for 9 buttons on this band – first 2 to come level with buttonholes already worked in right front, last to come 1 cm above neck shaping and rem 6 evenly spaced between.
Buttonhole band
Slip 7 sts from right front holder onto 2¾mm (US 2) needles and rejoin yarn A with WS facing.
Cont in rib as set until band, when slightly stretched, fits up right front opening edge to neck shaping, ending with a WS row and with the addition of a further 6 buttonholes worked to correspond with positions marked for buttons as folls:

Buttonhole row (RS): K1, P1, K2tog, yfwd (to make a buttonhole), rib 3.
Do NOT break off yarn.
Slip stitch band in place.
Neckband
With RS facing, using 2¾mm (US 2) needles and yarn A, rib across 7 sts of buttonhole band, pick up and knit 33 (34: 34: 36: 36) sts up right side of neck, 45 (47: 47: 49: 49) sts from back, and 33 (34: 34: 36: 36) sts down left side of neck, then rib across 7 sts of button band. 125 (129: 129: 135: 135) sts.
Keeping rib correct as set by bands, work in rib for 3 rows, ending with a WS row.
Row 4 (RS): K1, P1, K2tog, yfwd (to make 9th buttonhole), rib to end.
Work in rib for a further 3 rows.
Cast off in rib.
See information page for finishing instructions, setting in sleeves using the set-in method.

JOSEPH

KIM HARGREAVES

YARN

	S	M	L	XL	XXL
To fit chest	97	102	107	112	117 cm
	38	40	42	44	46 in

Rowan Yorkshire Tweed Chunky

| 9 | 9 | 10 | 10 | 11 x 100gm |

(photographed in Rivet 552)

NEEDLES
1 pair 7mm (no 2) (US 10½) needles
1 pair 8mm (no 0) (US 11) needles
Cable needle

TENSION
12 sts and 16 rows to 10 cm measured over stocking stitch using 8mm (US 11) needles.

SPECIAL ABBREVIATIONS
Cr2L = Cross 2 left Slip next st onto cable needle and leave at front of work, P1, then K1 from cable needle
Cr2R = Cross 2 right Slip next st onto cable needle and leave at back of work, K1, then P1 from cable needle
C2B = Cable 2 back Slip next st onto cable needle and leave at back of work, K1, then K1 from cable needle
C2F = Cable 2 front Slip next st onto cable needle and leave at front of work, K1, then K1 from cable needle
C4B = Cable 4 back Slip next 2 sts onto cable needle and leave at back of work, K2, then K2 from cable needle
C4F = Cable 4 front Slip next 2 sts onto cable needle and leave at front of work, K2, then K2 from cable needle
Cr3L = Cross 3 left Slip next 2 sts onto cable needle and leave at front of work, P1, then K2 from cable needle
Cr3R = Cross 3 right Slip next st onto cable needle and leave at back of work, K2, then P1 from cable needle
C5B = Cable 5 back Slip next 3 sts onto cable needle and leave at back of work, K2, slip P st from cable needle back onto left needle and P this st, then K2 from cable needle

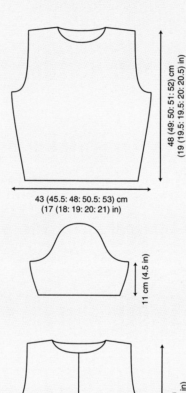

48 (49: 50: 51: 52) cm
(19 (19.5: 19.5: 20: 20.5) in)

43 (45.5: 48: 50.5: 53) cm
(17 (18: 19: 20: 21) in)

11 cm (4.5 in)

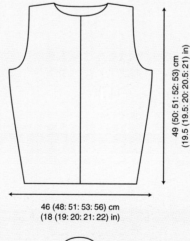

49 (50: 51: 52: 53) cm
(19.5 (19.5: 20: 20.5: 21) in)

46 (48: 51: 53: 56) cm
(18 (19: 20: 21: 22) in)

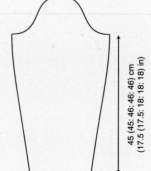

45 (45: 46: 46: 46) cm
(17.5 (17.5: 18: 18: 18) in)

BACK

Cast on 77 (79: 83: 85: 89) sts using 7mm (US 10½) needles.

Row 1 (RS): P0 (1: 0: 0: 0), K2 (2: 1: 2: 0), (P2, K2) 9 (9: 10: 10: 11) times, P1, (K2, P2) 9 (9: 10: 10: 11) times, K2 (2: 1: 2: 0), P0 (1: 0: 0: 0).

Row 2: K0 (1: 0: 0: 0), P2 (2: 1: 2: 0), (K2, P2) 9 (9: 10: 10: 11) times, K1, (P2, K2) 9 (9: 10: 10: 11) times, P2 (2: 1: 2: 0), K0 (1: 0: 0: 0).

These 2 rows form rib.

Work in rib for a further 13 rows, ending with a RS row.

Row 16 (WS): Rib 12 (13: 15: 16: 18), M1, rib 2, M1, rib 5, M1, rib 3, (M1, rib 2) 3 times, M1, rib 21, M1, (rib 2, M1) 3 times, rib 3, M1, rib 5, M1, rib 2, M1, rib to end. 91 (93: 97: 99: 103) sts.

Change to 8mm (US 11) needles.

Starting and ending rows as indicated, working rows 1 and 2 once only and then repeating rows 3 to 26 throughout, cont in patt from chart for back until back measures 43 (43: 44: 44: 45) cm, ending with a WS row.

Shape armholes

Keeping patt correct, cast off 3 sts at beg of next 2 rows. 85 (87: 91: 93: 97) sts.

Dec 1 st at each end of next 2 rows. 81 (83: 87: 89: 93) sts.

Cont straight until armhole measures 24 (25: 25: 26: 26) cm, ending with a WS row.

Shape shoulders and back neck

Cast off 9 (9: 9: 9: 10) sts at beg of next 2 rows. 63 (65: 69: 71: 73) sts.

Next row (RS): Cast off 9 (9: 9: 9: 10) sts, patt until there are 11 (11: 13: 13: 13) sts on right needle and turn, leaving rem sts on a holder.

Work each side of neck separately.

Cast off 3 sts at beg of next row.

Cast off rem 8 (8: 10: 10: 10) sts.

With RS facing, rejoin yarn to rem sts, cast off centre 23 (25: 25: 27: 27) sts, patt to end.

Complete to match first side, reversing shapings.

FRONT

Work as given for back until 10 (10: 12: 12: 12) rows less have been worked than on back to start of shoulder shaping, ending with a WS row.

Shape neck

Next row (RS): Patt 33 (33: 36: 36: 38) sts and turn, leaving rem sts on a holder.

Work each side of neck separately.

Dec 1 st at neck edge of next 5 rows, then on foll 2 (2: 3: 3: 3) alt rows, ending with a WS row. 26 (26: 28: 28: 30) sts.

Shape shoulder

Cast off 9 (9: 9: 9: 10) sts at beg of next and foll alt row.

Work 1 row. Cast off rem 8 (8: 10: 10: 10) sts.

With RS facing, rejoin yarn to rem sts, cast off centre 15 (17: 15: 17: 17) sts, patt to end.

Complete to match first side, reversing shapings.

SLEEVES (both alike)

Cast on 40 (40: 40: 42: 42) sts using 7mm (US 10½) needles.

Row 1 (RS): K1 (1: 1: 2: 2), ★P2, K2, rep from ★ to last 3 (3: 3: 4: 4) sts, P2, K1 (1: 1: 2: 2).

Row 2: P1 (1: 1: 2: 2), ★K2, P2, rep from ★ to last 3 (3: 3: 4: 4) sts, K2, P1 (1: 1: 2: 2).

These 2 rows form rib.

Work in rib for a further 13 rows, ending with a RS row.

Row 16 (WS): Rib 9 (9: 9: 10: 10), M1, rib 2, M1, rib 4, M1, rib 2, M1, rib 6, M1, rib 2, M1, rib 4, M1, rib 2, M1, rib to end. 48 (48: 48: 50: 50) sts.

Change to 8mm (US 11) needles.

Starting and ending rows as indicated, working rows 1 and 2 once only and then repeating rows 3 to 14 throughout, cont in patt from chart for sleeves, shaping sides by inc 1 st at each end of 3rd and every foll 6th (4th: 4th: 6th: 6th) row to 66 (52: 52: 70: 70) sts, then on every foll – (6th: 6th: –: –) row until there are – (68: 68: –: –) sts, taking inc sts into patt.

Cont straight until sleeve measures 49 (50: 50: 51: 51) cm, ending with a WS row.

Shape top

Keeping patt correct, cast off 3 sts at beg of next 2 rows. 60 (62: 62: 64: 64) sts.

Dec 1 st at each end of next and foll alt row.

Work 1 row, ending with a WS row.

Cast off rem 56 (58: 58: 60: 60) sts.

MAKING UP

PRESS as described on the information page. Join right shoulder seam using back stitch, or mattress st if preferred.

Neckband

With RS facing and using 7mm (US 10½) needles, pick up and knit 14 (14: 15: 15: 17) sts down left side of neck, 11 (13: 11: 13: 13) sts from front, 14 (14: 15: 15: 17) sts up right side of neck, then 25 (27: 27: 29: 29) sts from back. 64 (68: 68: 72: 76) sts.

Row 1 (WS): ★P2, K2, rep from ★ to end.

Rep this row until neckband measures 9 cm. Cast off in rib.

See information page for finishing instructions, setting in sleeves using the shallow set-in method.

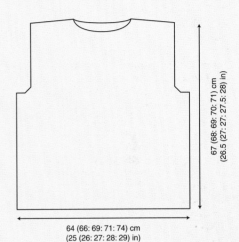

67 (68: 69: 70: 71) cm
(26.5 (27: 27: 27.5: 28) in)

64 (66: 69: 71: 74) cm
(25 (26: 27: 28: 29) in)

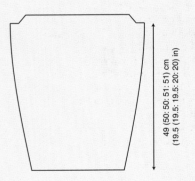

49 (50: 50: 51: 51) cm
(19.5 (19.5: 19.5: 20: 20) in)

Sleeve chart

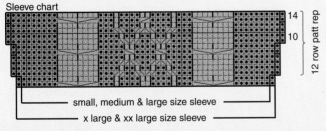

14
10

12 row patt rep

small, medium & large size sleeve
x large & xx large size sleeve

Back chart

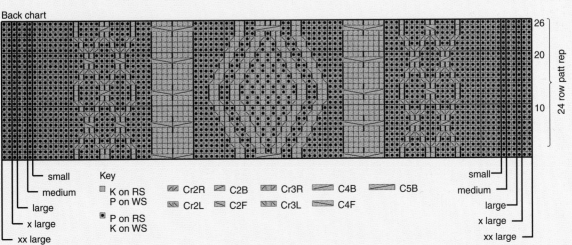

26
20
10

24 row patt rep

small
medium
large
x large
xx large

small
medium
large
x large
xx large

Key
K on RS P on WS
P on RS K on WS

Cr2R C2B Cr3R C4B C5B
Cr2L C2F Cr3L C4F

Design number 8

MERRY

KIM HARGREAVES

YARN

	XS	S	M	L	XL	
To fit bust	81	86	91	97	102	cm
	32	34	36	38	40	in

Rowan Yorkshire Tweed DK and 4 ply

A DK Revel	342	10	11	11	12	12 x 50gm
B 4 ply Cheerful	271	1	1	1	1	1 x 25gm
C 4 ply Brilliant	274	1	1	1	1	1 x 25gm

NEEDLES

1 pair 3¼mm (no 10) (US 3) needles
1 pair 4mm (no 8) (US 6) needles

BUTTONS

4 x 75319

TENSION

20 sts and 28 rows to 10 cm measured over
stocking stitch using 4mm (US 6) needles and
yarn A.

SPECIAL ABBREVIATIONS

Tuck 4 (5: 6: 7: 8) = Form tuck by picking up
corresponding st 4 (5: 6: 7: 8) rows below (see
pattern note below).

Pattern note: Tuck pattern is formed by
working next st together with corresponding st
4, 5, 6, 7 or 8 rows below.
On RS rows, insert right needle into next st on
left needle as though to K it, then through back
loop of same st 4 (5: 6: 7: 8) rows below, knitting
the 2 sts together.
On WS rows, insert right needle into next st on
left needle as though to P it, then through front
loop of same st 4 (5: 6: 7: 8) rows below, purling
the 2 sts together.

BACK

Cast on 91 (95: 101: 105: 111) sts using 3¼mm
(US 3) needles and yarn A.
Beg with a K row, work in st st for 10 rows,
ending with a WS row.
Change to 4mm (US 6) needles.
Cont in st st for a further 10 rows, ending with a
WS row.

Row 21 (RS): K28 (30: 32: 34: 36), tuck 5, K1,
tuck 6, K1, tuck 7, K1, (tuck 8, K1) 3 times, tuck
7, K1, tuck 5, K5 (5: 7: 7: 9), tuck 5, K1, tuck 7,
K1, (tuck 8, K1) 3 times, tuck 7, K1, tuck 6, K1,
tuck 5, K to end.
Work 3 rows.
Row 25: K4 (4: 5: 5: 6), ★tuck 5, K1, tuck 6, K1,
tuck 7, K1, (tuck 8, K1) twice, tuck 7, K1, tuck
6, K1, tuck 5★, K to last 19 (19: 20: 20: 21) sts,
rep from ★ to ★ once more, K to end.
Work 5 rows.
Row 31: K1, K2tog, K to last 3 sts, K2tog tbl,
K1. 89 (93: 99: 103: 109) sts.
Work 1 row.
Row 33: K17 (19: 21: 23: 25), tuck 5, K1, tuck
6, K1, tuck 7, K1, (tuck 8, K1) 3 times, tuck 7,
K1, tuck 6, K1, tuck 5, K1, tuck 4, K17 (17: 19:
19: 21), tuck 4, K1, tuck 5, K1, tuck 6, K1, tuck
7, K1, (tuck 8, K1) 3 times, tuck 7, K1, tuck 6,
K1, tuck 5, K to end.
Work 3 rows.
Row 37: As row 31. 87 (91: 97: 101: 107) sts.
Work 4 rows.
Row 42 (WS): P4 (4: 5: 5: 6), ★tuck 5, P1, tuck
6, P1, tuck 7, P1, (tuck 8, P1) twice, tuck 7, P1,
tuck 6, P1, tuck 5★, P to last 19 (19: 20: 20: 21) sts,
rep from ★ to ★ once more, P to end.
Work 2 rows.
Row 43: As row 31. 85 (89: 95: 99: 105) sts.
Work 2 rows.
Row 46 (WS): P25 (27: 29: 31: 33), ★tuck 5, P1,
tuck 6, P1, tuck 7, P1, (tuck 8, P1) twice, tuck 7,
P1, tuck 6, P1, tuck 5★, P5 (5: 7: 7: 9), rep from ★
to ★ once more, P to end.
Work 2 rows.
Row 49: As row 31. 83 (87: 93: 97: 103) sts.
Work 4 rows.
Row 54 (WS): P9 (9: 10: 10: 11), tuck 4, P1,
tuck 5, P1, tuck 6, P1, tuck 7, (P1, tuck 8) 3 times,
P1, tuck 7, P1, tuck 6, P1, tuck 5, P to last
28 (28: 29: 29: 30) sts, tuck 5, P1, tuck 6, P1,
tuck 7, (P1, tuck 8) 3 times, P1, tuck 7, P1,
tuck 6, P1, tuck 5, P1, tuck 4, P to end.
Working all side seam decreases as set by row 31,
dec 1 st at each end of next and every foll 6th
row until 77 (81: 87: 91: 97) sts rem.
Work 7 (9: 9: 11: 11) rows, ending with a WS
row.
Next row (RS): K2, M1, K to last 2 sts, M1, K2.
Working all increases as set by last row, inc 1 st
at each end of every foll 6th row until there are
91 (95: 101: 105: 111) sts.
Work a further 15 rows, ending with a WS row.
Shape armholes
Cast off 3 (4: 4: 5: 5) sts at beg of next 2 rows.
85 (87: 93: 95: 101) sts.
Dec 1 st at each end of next 5 (5: 7: 7: 9) rows,
then on foll 3 alt rows. 69 (71: 73: 75: 77) sts.
Cont straight until armhole measures 20 (20: 21:
21: 22) cm, ending with a WS row.
Shape shoulders and back neck
Cast off 7 (7: 7: 7: 8) sts at beg of next 2 rows.
55 (57: 59: 61: 61) sts.
Next row (RS): Cast off 7 (7: 7: 7: 8) sts, K until
there are 11 (11: 12: 12: 11) sts on right needle
and turn, leaving rem sts on a holder.
Work each side of neck separately.
Cast off 4 sts at beg of next row.
Cast off rem 7 (7: 8: 8: 7) sts.
With RS facing, rejoin yarn to rem sts, cast off
centre 19 (21: 21: 23: 23) sts, K to end.
Complete to match first side, reversing shapings.

LEFT FRONT

Cast on 46 (48: 51: 53: 56) sts using 3¼mm
(US 3) needles and yarn A.

Beg with a K row, work in st st for 10 rows,
ending with a WS row.
Change to 4mm (US 6) needles.
Cont in st st for a further 10 rows, ending with a
WS row.
Row 21 (RS): K28 (30: 32: 34: 36), tuck 5, K1,
tuck 6, K1, tuck 7, K1, (tuck 8, K1) 3 times,
tuck 7, K1, tuck 5, K to end.
Work 3 rows.
Row 25: K4 (4: 5: 5: 6), tuck 5, K1, tuck 6, K1,
tuck 7, K1, (tuck 8, K1) twice, tuck 7, K1,
tuck 6, K1, tuck 5, K to end.
Work 5 rows.
Row 31: K1, K2tog, K to end.
45 (47: 50: 52: 55) sts.
Work 1 row.
Row 33: K17 (19: 21: 23: 25), tuck 5, K1, tuck 6,
K1, tuck 7, K1, (tuck 8, K1) 3 times, tuck 7, K1,
tuck 6, K1, tuck 5, K1, tuck 4, K to end.
Work 3 rows.
Row 37: As row 31. 44 (46: 49: 51: 54) sts.
Work 4 rows.
Row 42 (WS): P to last 19 (19: 20: 20: 21) sts,
tuck 5, P1, tuck 6, P1, tuck 7, P1, (tuck 8, P1)
twice, tuck 7, P1, tuck 6, P1, tuck 5, P to end.
Row 43: As row 31. 43 (45: 48: 50: 53) sts.
Work 2 rows.
Row 46 (WS): P3 (3: 4: 4: 5), tuck 5, P1, tuck 6,
P1, tuck 7, P1, (tuck 8, P1) twice, tuck 7, P1,
tuck 6, P1, tuck 5, P to end.
Work 2 rows.
Row 49: As row 31. 42 (44: 47: 49: 52) sts.
Work 4 rows.
Row 54 (WS): P to last 28 (28: 29: 29: 30) sts,
tuck 5, P1, tuck 6, P1, tuck 7, (P1, tuck 8) 3 times,
P1, tuck 7, P1, tuck 6, P1, tuck 5, P1, tuck 4,
P to end.
Working all side seam decreases as set by row 31,
dec 1 st at beg of next and every foll 6th row
until 39 (41: 44: 46: 49) sts rem.
Work 7 (9: 9: 11: 11) rows, ending with a WS
row.
Next row (RS): K2, M1, K to end.
Working all increases as set by last row, inc 1 st at
beg of every foll 6th row until there are 46 (48:
51: 53: 56) sts.
Work 1 row, ending with a WS row.
Shape front slope
Dec 1 st at end of next and every foll 4th row
until 42 (44: 47: 49: 52) sts rem.
Work 1 row, ending with a WS row.
Shape armhole
Cast off 3 (4: 4: 5: 5) sts at beg of next row.
39 (40: 43: 44: 47) sts.
Work 1 row.
Dec 1 st at armhole edge of next 5 (5: 7: 7: 9) rows,
then on foll 3 alt rows **and at same time** dec 1 st
at front slope edge of next and every foll 4th row.
28 (29: 29: 30: 31) sts.
Dec 1 st at front slope edge **only** on 2nd (2nd:
4th: 4th: 2nd) and every foll 4th row to 26 (24:
26: 24: 27) sts, then on every foll 6th row until
21 (21: 22: 22: 23) sts rem.
Cont straight until left front matches back to
start of shoulder shaping, ending with a WS row.
Shape shoulder
Cast off 7 (7: 7: 7: 8) sts at beg of next and foll
alt row.
Work 1 row. Cast off rem 7 (7: 8: 8: 7) sts.

RIGHT FRONT

Cast on 46 (48: 51: 53: 56) sts using 3¼mm
(US 3) needles and yarn A.
Beg with a K row, work in st st for 10 rows,
ending with a WS row.

Change to 4mm (US 6) needles.
Cont in st st for a further 10 rows, ending with a WS row.
Row 21 (RS): K3 (3: 4: 4: 5), tuck 5, K1, tuck 7, K1, (tuck 8, K1) 3 times, tuck 7, K1, tuck 6, K1, tuck 5, K to end.
Work 3 rows.
Row 25: K to last 19 (19: 20: 20: 21) sts, tuck 5, K1, tuck 6, K1, tuck 7, K1, (tuck 8, K1) twice, tuck 7, K1, tuck 6, K1, tuck 5, K to end.
Work 5 rows.
Row 31: K to last 3 sts, K2tog tbl, K1.
45 (47: 50: 52: 55) sts.
Work 1 row.
Row 33: K9 (9: 10: 10: 11), tuck 4, K1, tuck 5, K1, tuck 6, K1, tuck 7, K1, (tuck 8, K1) 3 times, tuck 7, K1, tuck 6, K1, tuck 5, K to end.
Work 3 rows.
Row 37: As row 31. 44 (46: 49: 51: 54) sts.
Work 4 rows.
Row 42 (WS): P4 (4: 5: 5: 6), tuck 5, P1, tuck 6, P1, tuck 7, P1, (tuck 8, P1) twice, tuck 7, P1, tuck 6, P1, tuck 5, P to end.
Row 43: As row 31. 43 (45: 48: 50: 53) sts.
Work 2 rows.
Row 46 (WS): P25 (27: 29: 31: 33), tuck 5, P1, tuck 6, P1, tuck 7, P1, (tuck 8, P1) twice, tuck 7, P1, tuck 6, P1, tuck 5, P to end.
Work 2 rows.
Row 49: As row 31. 42 (44: 47: 49: 52) sts.
Work 4 rows.
Row 54 (WS): P9 (9: 10: 10: 11), tuck 4, P1, tuck 5, P1, tuck 6, P1, tuck 7, (P1, tuck 8) 3 times, P1, tuck 7, P1, tuck 6, P1, tuck 5, P to end.
Working all side seam decreases as set by row 31, dec 1 st at end of next and every foll 6th row until 39 (41: 44: 46: 49) sts rem.
Work 1 (3: 3: 5: 5) rows, ending with a WS row.
Next row (buttonhole row) (RS): K2, K2tog, yfwd, K to end.
Working a further 3 buttonholes in this way on every foll 14th row, cont as folls:
Work 5 rows, ending with a WS row.
Next row (RS): K to last 2 sts, M1, K2.
Complete to match left front, reversing shapings.

SLEEVES (both alike)
Cast on 53 (53: 55: 57: 57) sts using 3¼mm (US 3) needles and yarn A.
Beg with a K row, work in st st for 10 rows, ending with a WS row.
Place markers at both ends of last row.
Change to 4mm (US 6) needles.
Cont in st st for a further 10 rows, ending with a WS row.
Row 21 (RS): K5, tuck 6, K1, tuck 7, (K1, tuck 8) twice, K1, tuck 7, K1, tuck 6, K1, tuck 5, K to last 18 sts, tuck 5, K1, tuck 6, K1, tuck 7, (K1, tuck 8) twice, K1, tuck 7, K1, tuck 6, K to end.
Work 3 rows.
Row 25: K2, M1, K to last 2 sts, M1, K2.
55 (55: 57: 59: 59) sts.
Working all increases as set by this row, cont as folls:
Work 5 rows.
Rows 31: K19 (19: 20: 21: 21), tuck 5, K1, tuck 6, K1, tuck 7, (K1, tuck 8) 3 times, K1, tuck 7, K1, tuck 6, K1, tuck 5, K to end.
Work 9 rows, inc 0 (0: 0: 0: 1) st at each end of 8th of these rows. 55 (55: 57: 59: 61) sts.
Row 41: (K2, M1) 0 (1: 1: 1: 0) times, K5 (3: 4: 5: 8), *tuck 5, K1, tuck 6, K1, tuck 7, (K1, tuck 8) 3 times, K1, tuck 7, K1, tuck 6, K1, tuck 5*, K11, rep from * to * once more, K to last 0 (2: 2: 2: 0) sts, (M1, K2) 0 (1: 1: 1: 0) times.
55 (57: 59: 61: 61) sts.

Work 9 rows, inc 1 (0: 0: 0: 0) st at each end of 2nd of these rows.
57 (57: 59: 61: 61) sts.
Row 51: K20 (20: 21: 22: 22), tuck 5, K1, tuck 6, K1, tuck 7, (K1, tuck 8) 3 times, K1, tuck 7, K1, tuck 6, K1, tuck 5, K to end.
Beg with a P row, cont in st st, inc 1 st at each end of 10th (6th: 6th: 6th: 2nd) and every foll 18th (16th: 16th: 16th: 14th) row to 63 (61: 65: 67: 69) sts, then on every foll 16th (14th: 14th: 14th: 12th) row until there are 67 (69: 71: 73: 75) sts.
Cont straight until sleeve measures 43 (43: 44: 44: 44) cm **from markers**, ending with a WS row.
Shape top
Cast off 3 (4: 4: 5: 5) sts at beg of next 2 rows.
61 (61: 63: 63: 65) sts.
Dec 1 st at each end of next 3 rows, then on foll 2 alt rows, then on every foll 4th row until 39 (39: 41: 41: 43) sts rem.
Work 1 row.
Dec 1 st at each end of next and every foll alt row until 33 sts rem, then on foll 3 rows, ending with a WS row.
Cast off rem 27 sts.

MAKING UP
PRESS as described on the information page.
Join both shoulder seams using back stitch, or mattress st if preferred.
Collar (make 2)
Cast on 5 sts using 4mm (US 6) needles and yarn A.
Beg with a K row, work in st st as folls:
Work 1 row.
Inc 1 st at each end of next 8 rows, then on foll 10 alt rows. 41 sts.
Work 1 row, ending with a WS row.
Row 31 (RS): Inc in first st, K9, (tuck 5, K1) twice, tuck 6, K1, tuck 7, (K1, tuck 8) 3 times, K1, tuck 7, K1, tuck 6, (K1, tuck 5) twice, K to last st, inc in last st. 43 sts.
Inc 1 st at each end of 2nd and foll 5 alt rows, then on foll 4th row. 57 sts.
Row 48 (WS): P8, *tuck 5, P1, tuck 6, P1, tuck 7, P1, (tuck 8, P1) 3 times, tuck 7, P1, tuck 6, P1, tuck 5*, P7, rep from * to * once more, P to end.
Work 12 rows, inc 1 st at each end of 3rd and every foll 4th row. 63 sts.
Row 61: K19, tuck 5, K1, tuck 6, (K1, tuck 7) twice, (K1, tuck 8) 5 times, (K1, tuck 7) twice, K1, tuck 6, K1, tuck 5, K to end.
Work 12 rows, inc 1 st at each end of 2nd and every foll 4th row. 69 sts.
Row 74 (WS): P10, *tuck 5, P1, tuck 6, P1, tuck 7, (P1, tuck 8) 3 times, P1, tuck 7, P1, tuck 6, P1, tuck 5*, P15, rep from * to * once more, P to end.
Work 12 rows, inc 1 st at each end of first of these rows. 71 sts.
Row 87: K21, tuck 5, K1, tuck 6, (K1, tuck 7) twice, (K1, tuck 8) 7 times, (K1, tuck 7) twice, K1, tuck 6, K1, tuck 5, K to end.
Work 13 rows.
Row 101: K7, *tuck 5, K1, tuck 6, K1, tuck 7, (K1, tuck 8) 3 times, K1, tuck 7, K1, tuck 6, K1, tuck 5*, K23, rep from * to * once more, K to end.
Cont straight until collar, unstretched, fits from start of front slope shaping to centre back neck, ending with a WS row.
Cast off.
Join centre back (cast-off) seam of collars, then sew one edge to front slope and back neck edges,

positioning cast-on edges at start of front slope shaping. Fold collar in half to inside and slip stitch in place.
Left front facing
With RS facing, using 3¼mm (US 3) needles and yarn A, beg at start of front slope shaping, pick up and knit 65 (67: 67: 69: 69) sts evenly down left front opening edge, ending 20 rows up from cast-on edge.
Beg with a P row, work in st st for 7 rows, inc 1 st at front slope edge of 2nd and foll 2 alt rows.
68 (70: 70: 72: 72) sts.
Cast off.
Right front facing
With RS facing, using 3¼mm (US 3) needles and yarn A, beg 20 rows up from cast-on edge, pick up and knit 65 (67: 67: 69: 69) sts evenly up right front opening edge, ending at start of front slope shaping.
Work as given for left front facing, with the addition of 4 buttonholes in row 2, worked by replacing "K2" level with buttonholes already worked in right front with "K2tog, yfwd".
Fold facings to inside and slip stitch in place.
See information page for finishing instructions, setting in sleeves using the set-in method. Fold first 10 rows to inside around lower edge of body and sleeves and slip stitch in place.
Embroidery
Following photograph as a guide, embroider flowers at random over tuck patterned areas as folls: using yarn B, work a large french knot for each flower centre. Using yarn C, work 4 bullion knots radiating out from flower centre to form petals.

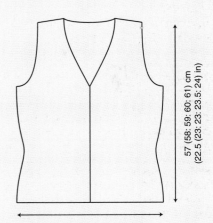

45.5 (47.5: 50.5: 52.5: 55.5) cm
(18 (18.5: 20: 20.5: 22) in)

57 (58: 59: 60: 61) cm
(22.5 (23: 23: 23.5: 24) in)

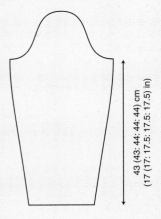

43 (43: 44: 44: 44) cm
(17 (17: 17.5: 17.5: 17.5) in)

TINY FLOWER

SASHA KAGAN

YARN

	XS	S	M	L	XL	
To fit bust	81	86	91	97	102 cm	
	32	34	36	38	40 in	

Rowan Yorkshire Tweed 4 ply

A Feral	284	10	11	12	12	13	x 25gm
B Highlander	266	1	1	1	1	1	x 25gm
C Blessed	269	1	1	1	1	1	x 25gm
D Glory	273	1	1	1	1	1	x 25gm
E Radiant	276	1	1	1	1	1	x 25gm
F Foxy	275	2	2	2	2	2	x 25gm

NEEDLES

1 pair 2¼mm (no 13) (US 1) needles
1 pair 3mm (no 11) (US 2/3) needles
Cable needle
2.50mm (no 12) (US C2) crochet hook

BUTTONS - 9 x 75322

TENSION

28 sts and 40 rows to 10 cm measured over
stocking stitch using 3mm (US 2/3) needles.

SPECIAL ABBREVIATIONS

C4B = Cable 4 back Slip next 2 sts onto cn
and leave at back of work, K2, then K2 from cn

CROCHET ABBREVIATIONS

ss = slip stitch; **ch** = chain; **dc** = double crochet;
tr = treble; **sp** = space.

BACK

Cast on 124 (130: 138: 144: 152) sts using 3mm
(US 2/3) needles and yarn A.
Using the **intarsia** technique as described on
the information page, starting and ending rows
as indicated and repeating the 80 row repeat
throughout, cont in patt from chart as folls:
Work 8 rows, ending with a WS row.
Dec 1 st at each end of next and every foll 6th
row until 114 (120: 128: 134: 142) sts rem.
Work 17 rows, ending with a WS row.
Inc 1 st at each end of next and every foll 12th
row until there are 124 (130: 138: 144: 152) sts,
taking inc sts into patt.

Cont straight until back measures 29 (30: 30: 31:
31) cm, ending with a WS row.
Shape armholes
Keeping patt correct, cast off 7 (8: 8: 9: 9) sts at
beg of next 2 rows. 110 (114: 122: 126: 134) sts.
Dec 1 st at each end of next 5 (5: 7: 7: 9) rows,
then on foll 1 (2: 2: 3: 3) alt rows, then on every
foll 4th row until 94 (96: 100: 102: 106) sts rem.
Cont straight until armhole measures 20 (20: 21:
21: 22) cm, ending with a WS row.
Shape shoulders and back neck
Cast off 8 (8: 9: 9: 10) sts at beg of next 2 rows.
78 (80: 82: 84: 86) sts.
Next row (RS): Cast off 8 (8: 9: 9: 10) sts, patt
until there are 13 sts on right needle and turn,
leaving rem sts on a holder.
Work each side of neck separately.
Cast off 4 sts at beg of next row.
Cast off rem 9 sts.
With RS facing, rejoin yarn to rem sts, cast off
centre 36 (38: 38: 40: 40) sts, patt to end.
Complete to match first side, reversing shapings.

LEFT FRONT

Cast on 64 (67: 71: 74: 78) sts using 3mm (US
2/3) needles and yarn A.
Starting and ending rows as indicated and
repeating the 80 row repeat throughout, cont in
patt from chart as folls:
(**Note**: do **NOT** work part flower or cable
motifs along front opening edge.)
Work 8 rows, ending with a WS row.
Dec 1 st at beg of next and every foll 6th row
until 59 (62: 66: 69: 73) sts rem.
Work 17 rows, ending with a WS row.
Inc 1 st at beg of next and every foll 12th row
until there are 64 (67: 71: 74: 78) sts, taking inc sts
into patt.
Cont straight until left front matches back to
beg of armhole shaping, ending with a WS row.
Shape armhole
Keeping patt correct, cast off 7 (8: 8: 9: 9) sts at
beg of next row. 57 (59: 63: 65: 69) sts.
Work 1 row.
Dec 1 st at armhole edge of next 5 (5: 7: 7: 9) rows,
then on foll 1 (2: 2: 3: 3) alt rows, then on every
foll 4th row until 49 (50: 52: 53: 55) sts rem.
Cont straight until 21 (21: 21: 23: 23) rows less
have been worked than on back to start of
shoulder shaping, ending with a RS row.
Shape neck
Keeping patt correct, cast off 9 (10: 10: 10: 10) sts
at beg of next row, then 6 sts at beg of foll alt row.
34 (34: 36: 37: 39) sts.
Dec 1 st at neck edge of next 5 rows, then on
foll 3 (3: 3: 4: 4) alt rows, then on foll 4th row.
25 (25: 27: 27: 29) sts.
Work 3 rows, ending with a WS row.
Shape shoulder
Cast off 8 (8: 9: 9: 10) sts at beg of next and foll
alt row.
Work 1 row. Cast off rem 9 sts.

RIGHT FRONT

Cast on 64 (67: 71: 74: 78) sts using 3mm (US
2/3) needles and yarn A.
Starting and ending rows as indicated and
repeating the 80 row repeat throughout, cont in
patt from chart as folls:
(**Note**: do **NOT** work part flower or cable
motifs along front opening edge.)
Work 8 rows, ending with a WS row.
Dec 1 st at end of next and every foll 6th row
until 59 (62: 66: 69: 73) sts rem.
Complete to match left front, reversing shapings.

SLEEVES (both alike)

Cast on 64 (64: 66: 68: 68) sts using 3mm (US
2/3) needles and yarn A.
Starting and ending rows as indicated and
repeating the 80 row repeat throughout, cont in
patt from chart, shaping sides by inc 1 st at each
end of 7th and every foll 8th (8th: 8th: 8th: 6th)
row to 70 (80: 88: 90: 72) sts, then on every foll
10th (10th: 10th: 10th: 8th) row until there are
94 (96: 100: 102: 106) sts, taking inc sts into patt.
Cont straight until sleeve measures 41 (41: 42:
42: 42) cm, ending with a WS row.
Shape top
Keeping patt correct, cast off 7 (8: 8: 9: 9) sts at
beg of next 2 rows. 80 (80: 84: 84: 88) sts.
Dec 1 st at each end of next 5 rows, then on
foll 2 alt rows, then on every foll 4th row until
54 (54: 58: 58: 62) sts rem.
Work 1 row, ending with a WS row.
Dec 1 st at each end of next and every foll alt
row to 42 sts, then on foll 7 rows, ending with a
WS row.
Cast off rem 28 sts.

MAKING UP

PRESS as described on the information page.
Join both shoulder seams using back stitch, or
mattress st if preferred.
Button band
With RS facing, using 2¼mm (US 1) needles
and yarn A, pick up and knit 127 (127: 127: 135:
135) sts evenly down left front opening edge,
between neck shaping and cast-on edge.
Work in garter st for 2 rows.
Cast off knitwise (on **WS**).
Buttonhole band
Work to match button band, picking up sts up
right front opening edge and with the addition
of 6 buttonholes worked in row 2 as folls:

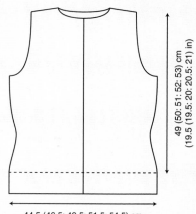

44.5 (46.5: 49.5: 51.5: 54.5) cm
(17.5 (18.5: 19.5: 20.5: 21.5) in)

49 (50: 51: 52: 53) cm
(19.5 (19.5: 20: 20.5: 21) in)

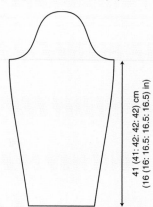

41 (41: 42: 42: 42) cm
(16 (16: 16.5: 16.5: 16.5) in)

Row 2 (RS): K2, ★K2tog, yfwd (to make a buttonhole), K13 (13: 13: 14: 14) rep from ★ to last 5 sts, K2tog, yfwd (to make 9th buttonhole), K3.

Neckband

With RS facing, using 2.50mm (US C2) crochet hook and yarn F, starting and ending at cast-off edge of bands, work a row of ss evenly around entire neck edge, working a multiple of 4 sts plus 1 st, turn.

Row 1 (WS): 1 ch (does NOT count as st), 1 dc into first st, ★5 ch, miss 3 sts, 1 dc into next st, rep from ★ to end, turn.

Row 2: (2 dc, 3 ch, ss to last dc, 2 dc) into each ch sp to end, ending with ss to dc at beg of previous row.

Fasten off. Join side seams.

Hem edging

With RS facing, using 2.50mm (US C2) crochet hook and yarn F, starting and ending at cast-off edge of bands, work a row of ss evenly around entire hem edge, working a multiple of 4 sts plus 1 st, turn.

Row 1 (WS): 1 ch (does NOT count as st), 1 dc into first st, ★5 ch, miss 3 sts, 1 dc into next st, rep from ★ to end, turn.

Row 2: 5 ch, 1 dc into first ch sp, ★5 ch, 1 dc into next ch sp, rep from ★ to end, 2 ch, 1 tr into dc at beg of previous row, turn.

Row 3: 1 ch (does NOT count as st), 1 dc into tr at end of previous row, ★5 ch, 1 dc into next ch sp, rep from ★ to end, working last dc into 3rd of 5 ch at beg of previous row, turn.

Rows 4 to 7: As rows 2 and 3, twice.

Row 8: (2 dc, 3 ch, ss to last dc, 2 dc) into each ch sp to end, ending with ss to dc at beg of previous row.

Fasten off.

In same way, work edging along cast-on edge of sleeves.

See information page for finishing instructions, setting in sleeves using the set-in method.

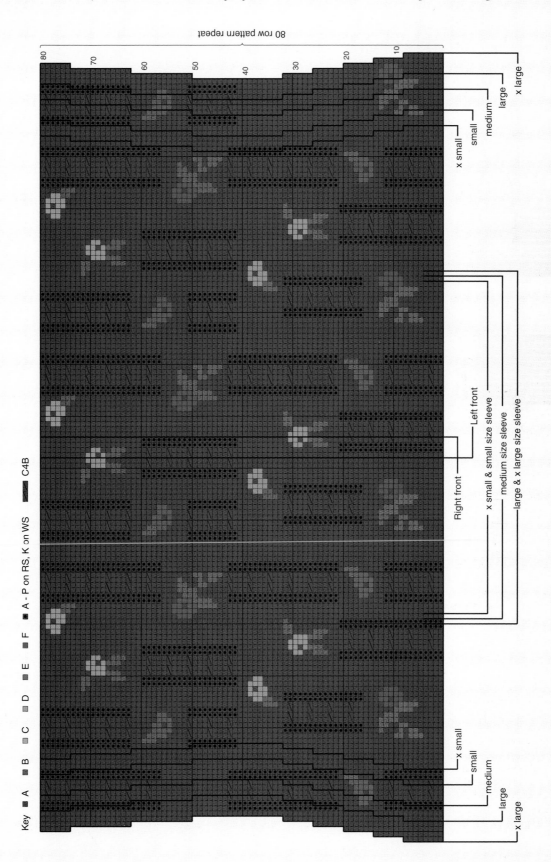

Design number 10

ERNEST

KIM HARGREAVES

YARN

	ladies			mens			
	S	M	L	M	L	XL	
To fit bust/chest	86	91	97	102	107	112	cm
	34	36	38	40	42	44	in

Rowan Magpie Aran

       8   8   9   9   9 10 x 100gm
(photographed in Boggy 690)

NEEDLES

1 pair 4mm (no 8) (US 6) needles
1 pair 5mm (no 6) (US 8) needles
Cable needle

TENSION

18 sts and 23 rows to 10 cm measured over
stocking stitch using 5mm (US 8) needles.

SPECIAL ABBREVIATIONS

C4B = Cable 4 back Slip next 2 sts onto cable
needle and leave at back of work, K2, then K2
from cable needle
C4F = Cable 4 front Slip next 2 sts onto cable
needle and leave at front of work, K2, then K2
from cable needle

Pattern note: The pattern is written for the 3
ladies sizes, followed by the mens sizes in **bold**.
Where only one figure appears this applies to all
sizes in that group.

BACK

Cast on 98 (98: 102: **106: 110: 114**) sts using
4mm (US 6) needles.
Row 1 (RS): K2, *P2, K2, rep from * to end.
Row 2: P2, *K2, P2, rep from * to end.
These 2 rows form rib.
Work in rib for a further 10 rows, inc 0 (1: 1: 1) st
at each end of last row and ending with a WS row.
98 (100: 104: **108: 112: 116**) sts.
Change to 5mm (US 8) needles.
Beg with a K row, cont in st st until back
measures 21 cm, ending with a RS row.
Next row (WS): P0 (1: 3: **5: 7: 9**), (M1) 0 (1: 1: **1**)
times, P2, M1, (P30, M1, P2, M1) twice, P30,
M1, P2, (M1) 0 (1: 1: **1**) times, P0 (1: 3: **5: 7: 9**).
104 (108: 112: **116: 120: 124**) sts.
Starting and ending rows as indicated and
repeating the 42 row repeat throughout, work in
patt from chart as folls:
Cont straight until back measures 43 cm, ending
with a WS row.
Shape armholes
Keeping patt correct, cast off 10 sts at beg of
next 2 rows. 84 (88: 92: **96: 100: 104**) sts.
Cont straight until armhole measures 22 (23: 24:
25: 26: 27) cm, ending with a WS row.
Shape shoulders and back neck
Cast off 8 (9: 9: **9: 10: 10**) sts at beg of next 2 rows.
68 (70: 74: **78: 80: 84**) sts.
Next row (RS): Cast off 8 (9: 9: **9: 10: 10**) sts,
patt until there are 13 (12: 13: **14: 13: 14**) sts on
right needle and turn, leaving rem sts on a
holder.

Work each side of neck separately.
Cast off 4 sts at beg of next row.
Cast off rem 9 (8: 9: **10: 9: 10**) sts.
With RS facing, rejoin yarn to rem sts, cast off
centre 26 (28: 30: **32: 34: 36**) sts, patt to end.
Complete to match first side, reversing shapings.

FRONT

Work as given for back until 10 (**12**) rows less
have been worked than on back to start of
shoulder shaping, ending with a WS row.
Shape neck
Next row (RS): Patt 33 (34: 35: **37: 38: 39**) sts
and turn, leaving rem sts on a holder.
Work each side of neck separately.
Dec 1 st at neck edge of next 8 rows, then on
foll 0 (**1**) alt rows.
25 (26: 27: **28: 29: 30**) sts.
Work 1 row, ending with a WS row.
Shape shoulder
Cast off 8 (9: 9: **9: 10: 10**) sts at beg of next and
foll alt row.
Work 1 row.
Cast off rem 9 (8: 9: **10: 9: 10**) sts.
With RS facing, rejoin yarn to rem sts, cast off
centre 18 (20: 22: **22: 24: 26**) sts, patt to end.
Complete to match first side, reversing shapings.

SLEEVES (both alike)

Cast on 50 (54: 54: **58: 58: 62**) sts using 4mm
(US 6) needles.
Work in rib as given for back for 12 rows,
ending with a WS row.
Change to 5mm (US 8) needles.
Beg with a K row, cont in st st, shaping sides by
inc 1 st at each end of 3rd and every foll
8th (8th: 6th: 8th: 6th: 6th) row to 56 (62: 72:
62: 78: 82) sts, then on every foll 6th (6th: -:
6th: -: -) row until there are 66 (70: -: **76:
-: -**) sts.
Next row (WS): P16 (18: 19: **21: 22: 24**), M1,
P2, M1, P30, M1, P2, M1, P to end.
70 (74: 76: **80: 82: 86**) sts.
Starting and ending rows as indicated and
repeating the 42 row repeat throughout, work in
patt from chart as folls:

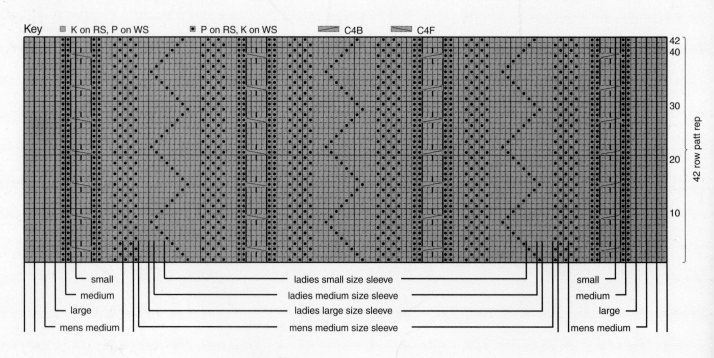

Key   ▨ K on RS, P on WS   ▣ P on RS, K on WS   C4B   C4F

42 40   30   20   10

42 row patt rep

small
medium
large
mens medium

ladies small size sleeve
ladies medium size sleeve
ladies large size sleeve
mens medium size sleeve

small
medium
large
mens medium

Inc 1 st at each end of 5th and every foll 6th row to 82 (86: 86: **94: 90: 96**) sts, then on every foll – (–: 4th: **–: 4th: 4th**) row until there are – (–: 90: **–: 98: 102**) sts, taking inc sts into patt.
Cont straight until sleeve measures 51 (52: 53: **55: 56: 57**) cm, ending with a **RS** row.
Cast off in patt.

MAKING UP
PRESS as described on the information page. Join right shoulder seam using back stitch, or mattress st if preferred.

Neckband
With RS facing and using 4mm (US 6) needles, pick up and knit 12 (**14**) sts down left side of neck, 18 (20: 22: **22: 24: 26**) sts from front, 12 (**14**) sts up right side of neck, then 40 (42: 44: **44: 46: 48**) sts from back.
82 (86: 90: **94: 98: 102**) sts.
Work in rib as given for back for 6 cm.
Cast off in rib.
See information page for finishing instructions, setting in sleeves using the square set-in method.

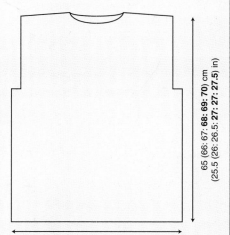

65 (66: 67: **68: 69: 70**) cm
(25.5 (26: 26.5: **27: 27: 27.5**) in)

54.5 (55.5: 58: **60: 62: 64.5**) cm
(21.5 (22: 23: **23.5: 24.5: 25.5**) in)

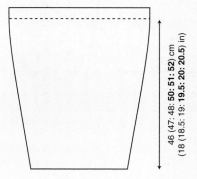

46 (47: 48: **50: 51: 52**) cm
(18 (18.5: 19: **19.5: 20: 20.5**) in)

MIST

KIM HARGREAVES

YARN
To fit average size adult head
Rowan Yorkshire Tweed 4 ply
Fairisle berets

	1st colourway		2nd colourway		
A	Butterscotch	272	Shrew	265	1 x25gm
B	Sheer	267	Sheer	267	1 x25gm
C	Oceanic	285	Highlander	266	1 x25gm
D	Graze	286	Butterscotch	272	1 x25gm
E	Glory	273	Foxy	275	1 x25gm
F	Brilliant	274	Blessed	269	1 x25gm
G	Foxy	275	Explode	277	1 x25gm
H	Mulled Wine	279	Radiant	276	1 x25gm

Striped beret

A	Knight	281	*Purple*	2 x25gm
B	Bristle	278	*blue*	1 x25gm

NEEDLES
1 pair 2¾mm (no 12) (US 2) needles
1 pair 3¼mm (no 10) (US 3) needles

TENSION
26 sts and 38 rows to 10 cm measured over stocking stitch using 3¼mm (US 3) needles.

Fairisle Beret
Cast on 146 sts using 2¾mm (US 2) needles and yarn B.
Break off yarn B and join in yarn A.
Row 1 (RS): K2, *P2, K2, rep from * to end.
Row 2: P2, *K2, P2, rep from * to end.
These 2 rows form rib.
Work in rib for a further 7 rows, ending with a RS row.
Row 10 (WS): Rib 2, *M1, rib 2, rep from * to end. 218 sts.
Change to 3¼mm (US 3) needles.★★
Using the **fairisle** technique as described on the information page, repeating the 12 st pattern repeat as required and working the edge sts as indicated on rows 7 to 9 and rows 34 to 36, cont in patt from chart, which is worked entirely in st st beg with a K row, as folls:
Work 28 rows.
Shape top
Keeping chart correct, cont as folls:

Row 29 (RS): *K4, K2tog, rep from * to last 2 sts, K2. 182 sts.
Work 13 rows.
Row 43: *K3, K2tog, rep from * to last 2 sts, K2. 146 sts.
Work 5 rows.
Row 49: *K2, K2tog, rep from * to last 2 sts, K2. 110 sts.
Work 3 rows.
Row 53: *K2tog, K1, rep from * to last 2 sts, K2tog. 73 sts.
Work 3 rows.
Row 57: *K2, K2tog, rep from * to last st, K1. 55 sts.
Work 1 row.
Row 59: *K2tog, rep from * to last st, K1. 28 sts.
Work 1 row.
Row 61: *K2tog, rep from * to end. 14 sts.
Work 1 row, ending with a WS row.
Break yarn and thread through rem 14 sts. Pull up tight and fasten off securely.

MAKING UP
Join back seam using back stitch, or mattress st if preferred. Cut a 28 cm disk of card and slip inside beret. **PRESS** as described on the info page.

Striped Beret
Work as given for fairisle beret to ★★.
Complete as given for fairisle beret, replacing chart with stripes as folls:
Rows 1 to 18: Using yarn A.
Rows 19 to 26: Using yarn B.
Rows 27 to 32: Using yarn A.
Rows 33 to 38: Using yarn B.
Rows 39 to 44: Using yarn A.
Rows 45 to 48: Using yarn B.
Rows 49 to 52: Using yarn A.
Rows 53 to 56: Using yarn B.
Rows 57 and 58: Using yarn A.
Rows 59 and 60: Using yarn B.
Rows 61 and 62: Using yarn A.

MAKING UP
Join back seam using back stitch, or mattress st if preferred. Cut a 28 cm disk of card and slip inside beret. **PRESS** as described on the information page. Make 5 cm diameter pompom using yarn A and attach to top of beret.

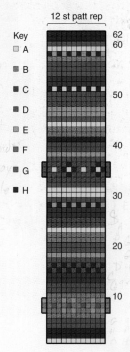

12 st patt rep

Key
□ A
■ B
■ C
■ D
■ E
■ F
■ G
■ H

62
60
50
40
30
20
10

BREEZE

KIM HARGREAVES

YARN

	ladies			mens		
	S	M	L	M	L	XL
To fit bust/chest	86	91	97	102	107	112 cm
	34	36	38	40	42	44 in

Rowan Magpie Aran

8 9 9 10 11 12 x 100gm

(ladies photographed in Truffle 320, mans in Toad 694)

NEEDLES

1 pair 4mm (no 8) (US 6) needles
1 pair 5mm (no 6) (US 8) needles
Cable needle

BUTTONS

7 x 75319

BUCKLE

Ladies version only: 2.5 cm (1 in) buckle

TENSION

18 sts and 23 rows to 10 cm measured over stocking stitch using 5mm (US 8) needles.

SPECIAL ABBREVIATIONS

Cr6R = Cross 6 right Slip next st onto cable needle and leave at back of work, (K1 tbl, P1) twice, K1 tbl, then P1 from cable needle
Cr6L = Cross 6 left Slip next 5 sts onto cable needle and leave at front of work, P1, then (K1 tbl, P1) twice, K1 tbl from cable needle
C11B = Cable 11 back Slip next 6 sts onto cable needle and leave at back of work, (K1 tbl, P1) twice, K1 tbl, then (P1, K1 tbl) 3 times from cable needle
C11F = Cable 11 front Slip next 5 sts onto cable needle and leave at front of work, (K1 tbl, P1) 3 times, then (K1 tbl, P1) twice, K1 tbl from cable needle

Pattern note: The pattern is written for the 3 ladies sizes, followed by the mens sizes in **bold**. Where only one figure appears this applies to all sizes in that group.

BACK

Cast on 103 (107: 111: **111: 115: 119**) sts using 4mm (US 6) needles.
Row 1 (RS): (K1 tbl, P1) 10 (11: 12: **10: 11: 12**) times, K1 tbl, P5, (K1 tbl, P1) 11 (**13**) times, K1 tbl, P5, K1 tbl, (P1, K1 tbl) 11 (**13**) times, P5, K1 tbl, (P1, K1 tbl) 10 (11: 12: **10: 11: 12**) times.
Row 2: (P1 tbl, K1) 10 (11: 12: **10: 11: 12**) times, P1 tbl, K5, (P1 tbl, K1) 11 (**13**) times, P1 tbl, K5, P1 tbl, (K1, P1 tbl) 11 (**13**) times, K5, P1 tbl, (K1, P1 tbl) 10 (11: 12: **10: 11: 12**) times.
These 2 rows form rib.
Work in rib for a further 22 rows, dec (**inc**) 1 st at each end of 19th of these rows and ending with a WS row. 101 (105: 109: **113: 117: 121**) sts.
Change to 5mm (US 8) needles.
Next row (RS): (P2tog) 1 (**0**) times, P13 (15: 17: **17: 19: 21**), *work next 15 sts as row 1 of cable chart for back, P13 (**17**), rep from * once more, work next 15 sts as row 1 of cable chart for back, P to last 2 (**0**) sts, (P2tog) 1 (**0**) times.
99 (103: 107: **113: 117: 121**) sts.
Next row: K14 (16: 18: **17: 19: 21**), *work next 15 sts as row 2 of cable chart for back, K13 (**17**), rep from * once more, work next 15 sts as row 2 of cable chart for back, K to end.
These 2 rows set the sts – 3 cable panels worked on rev st st.
Keeping sts correct as set, cont as folls:
Ladies sizes only
Dec 1 st at each end of 3rd and every foll 4th row until 93 (97: 101) sts rem.
All sizes
Work 7 (**10**) rows, ending with a WS row.
Inc 1 st at each end of next and every foll 6th (**16th**) row until there are 103 (107: 111: **119: 123: 127**) sts, taking inc sts into rev st st.
Cont straight until back measures 37 (**38**) cm, ending with a WS row.
Shape armholes
Keeping patt correct, cast off 4 (**5**) sts at beg of next 2 rows. 95 (99: 103: **109: 113: 117**) sts.
Dec 1 st at each end of next 5 rows, then on foll 4 alt rows. 77 (81: 85: **91: 95: 99**) sts.
Cont straight until armhole measures 20 (21: 22: **23: 24: 25**) cm, ending with a WS row.
Shape shoulders and back neck
Cast off 8 (8: 9: **9: 10: 10**) sts at beg of next 2 rows. 61 (65: 67: **73: 75: 79**) sts.
Next row (RS): Cast off 8 (8: 9: **9: 10: 10**) sts, patt until there are 11 (12: 12: **14: 13: 15**) sts on right needle and turn, leaving rem sts on a holder.
Work each side of neck separately.

Cast off 4 sts at beg of next row.
Cast off rem 7 (8: 8: **10: 9: 11**) sts.
With RS facing, rejoin yarn to rem sts, cast off centre 23 (25: 25: **27: 29: 29**) sts, patt to end.
Complete to match first side, reversing shapings.

LEFT FRONT

Cast on 55 (57: 59: **59: 61: 63**) sts using 4mm (US 6) needles.
Row 1 (RS): (K1 tbl, P1) 10 (11: 12: **10: 11: 12**) times, K1 tbl, P5, (K1 tbl, P1) 14 (**16**) times, K1 tbl.
Row 2: P1 tbl, (K1, P1 tbl) 14 (**16**) times, K5, P1 tbl, (K1, P1 tbl) 10 (11: 12: **10: 11: 12**) times.
These 2 rows form rib.
Mens sizes only
Work in rib for a further 2 rows.
Next row (buttonhole row) (RS): Rib to last 5 sts, work 2 tog, yrn, rib 3.
All sizes
Work in rib for a further 21 (**18**) rows, dec (**inc**) 1 st at beg of 19th (**16th**) of these rows and ending with a WS row.
54 (56: 58: **60: 62: 64**) sts.
Row 24 (WS): Rib 7 and slip these sts onto a holder, M1, rib to end. 48 (50: 52: **54: 56: 58**) sts.
Change to 5mm (US 8) needles.
Next row (RS): (P2tog) 1 (**0**) times, P13 (15: 17: **17: 19: 21**), work next 15 sts as row 1 of cable chart for back, P to end.
47 (49: 51: **54: 56: 58**) sts.
Next row: K18 (**22**), work next 15 sts as row 2 of cable chart for back, K to end.
These 2 rows set the sts – cable panel worked on rev st st.
Keeping sts correct as set, cont as folls:
Ladies sizes only
Dec 1 st at beg of 3rd and every foll 4th row until 44 (46: 48) sts rem.
All sizes
Work 7 (**10**) rows, ending with a WS row.
Inc 1 st at beg of next and every foll 6th (**16th**) row until there are 49 (51: 53: **57: 59: 61**) sts, taking inc sts into rev st st.
Cont straight until left front matches back to beg of armhole shaping, ending with a WS row.
Shape armhole
Keeping patt correct, cast off 4 (**5**) sts at beg of next row. 45 (47: 49: **52: 54: 56**) sts.
Work 1 row.
Dec 1 st at armhole edge of next 5 rows, then on foll 4 alt rows. 36 (38: 40: **43: 45: 47**) sts.
Cont straight until 15 (**17**) rows less have been worked than on back to start of shoulder shaping, ending with a RS row.
Shape neck
Keeping patt correct, cast off 5 (6: 6: **7: 8: 8**) sts at beg of next row. 31 (32: 34: **36: 37: 39**) sts.
Dec 1 st at neck edge of next 6 rows, then on foll 2 alt rows. 23 (24: 26: **28: 29: 31**) sts.
Work 4 (**6**) rows, ending with a WS row.
Shape shoulder
Cast off 8 (8: 9: **9: 10: 10**) sts at beg of next and foll alt row.
Work 1 row.
Cast off rem 7 (8: 8: **10: 9: 11**) sts.

RIGHT FRONT

Cast on 55 (57: 59: **59: 61: 63**) sts using 4mm (US 6) needles.
Row 1 (RS): K1 tbl, (P1, K1 tbl) 14 (**16**) times, P5, K1 tbl, (P1, K1 tbl) 10 (11: 12: **10: 11: 12**) times.
Row 2: (P1 tbl, K1) 10 (11: 12: **10: 11: 12**) times, P1 tbl, K5, (P1 tbl, K1) 14 (**16**) times, P1 tbl.
These 2 rows form rib.

Ladies sizes only
Work in rib for a further 2 rows.
Next row (buttonhole row) (RS): Rib 2, work 2 tog, yrn, rib to end.
All sizes
Work in rib for a further 18 (21) rows, dec (**inc**) 1 st at end of 16th (**19th**) of these rows and ending with a WS row. 54 (56: 58: **60: 62: 64**) sts.
Row 24 (WS): Rib to last 7 sts, M1 and turn, leaving last 7 sts on a holder.
48 (50: 52: **54: 56: 58**) sts.
Change to 5mm (US 8) needles.
Next row (RS): P18 (**22**), work next 15 sts as row 1 of cable chart for right front, P to last 2 (**0**) sts, (P2tog) 1 (**0**) times.
47 (49: 51: **54: 56: 58**) sts.
Next row: K14 (16: 18: **17: 19: 21**), work next 15 sts as row 2 of cable chart for right front, K to end.
These 2 rows set the sts - cable panel worked on rev st st.
Keeping sts correct as set, cont as folls:
Ladies sizes only
Dec 1 st at end of 3rd and every foll 4th row until 44 (46: 48) sts rem.
All sizes
Work 7 (**10**) rows, ending with a WS row.
Inc 1 st at end of next and every foll 6th (**16th**) row until there are 49 (51: 53: **57: 59: 61**) sts, taking inc sts into rev st st.
Complete to match left front, reversing shapings.

SLEEVES (both alike)
Cast on 53 (53: 57: **57: 61: 61**) sts using 4mm (US 6) needles.
Row 1 (RS): (P1, K1 tbl) 12 (12: 13: **13: 14: 14**) times, P5, (K1 tbl, P1) 12 (12: 13: **13: 14: 14**) times.
Row 2: (K1, P1 tbl) 12 (12: 13: **13: 14: 14**) times, K5, (P1 tbl, K1) 12 (12: 13: **13: 14: 14**) times.
These 2 rows form rib.
Work in rib for a further 14 rows, ending with a WS row.
Change to 5mm (US 8) needles.
Next row (RS): P19 (19: 21: **21: 23: 23**), work next 15 sts as row 1 of cable chart for back, P to end.
Next row: K19 (19: 21: **21: 23: 23**), work next 15 sts as row 2 of cable chart for back, K to end.

These 2 rows set the sts - cable panel worked on rev st st.
Keeping sts correct as set, cont as folls:
Inc 1 st at each end of next and every foll 18th (12th: 12th: **8th**) row to 59 (65: 71: **79: 83: 75**) sts, then on every foll 16th (10th: –: **6th**) row until there are 63 (67: –: **81: 85: 89**) sts, taking inc sts into rev st st.
Cont straight until sleeve measures 42 (43: 45: **50: 52: 53**) cm, ending with a WS row.
Shape top
Keeping patt correct, cast off 4 (**5**) sts at beg of next 2 rows. 55 (59: 63: **71: 75: 79**) sts.
Dec 1 st at each end of next 3 (**5**) rows, then on foll 2 (**5**) alt rows, then on every foll 4th row until 37 (41: 45: **45: 49: 53**) sts rem.
Work 1 row, ending with a WS row.
Dec 1 st at each end of next and foll 1 (**2**) alt rows, then on every row until 31 (**33**) sts rem, ending with a WS row. Cast off.

MAKING UP
PRESS as described on the information page. Join both shoulder seams using back stitch, or mattress st if preferred.
Button band
Ladies sizes only
Slip 7 sts from left front holder onto 4mm (US 6) needles and rejoin yarn with RS facing.
Mens sizes only
Slip 7 sts from right front holder onto 4mm (US 6) needles and rejoin yarn with WS facing.
All sizes
Cont in rib as set until band, when slightly stretched, fits up front opening edge to neck shaping. Cast off.
Slip stitch band in place.
Mark positions for 7 buttons on this band - first to come level with buttonhole already worked in other front, second to come immediately after rib, last to come 1.5 cm below neck shaping, and rem 4 buttons evenly spaced between.
Buttonhole band
Ladies sizes only
Slip 7 sts from right front holder onto 4mm (US 6) needles and rejoin yarn with WS facing.
Mens sizes only
Slip 7 sts from left front holder onto 4mm (US 6) needles and rejoin yarn with RS facing.

All sizes
Cont in rib as set until band, when slightly stretched, fits up front opening edge to neck shaping, with the addition of a further 6 buttonholes worked to correspond with positions marked for buttons as folls:
Buttonhole row (RS): Rib 2, work 2 tog, yrn, rib 3.
Cast off.
Slip stitch band in place.
Collar
Cast on 97 (99: 103: **105: 109: 111**) sts using 4mm (US 6) needles.
Row 1 (RS): K1 tbl, *P1, K1 tbl, rep from * to end.
Row 2: P1 tbl, *K1, P1 tbl, rep from * to end.
These 2 rows form rib.
Cont in rib until collar measures 10 (**13**) cm.
Cast off in rib.
Positioning ends of collar halfway across top of bands, stitch cast-on edge of collar to neck edge.
Ladies sizes only
Belt
Cast on 7 sts using 4mm (US 6) needles.
Work in rib as given for collar for 115 cm.
Cast off in rib.
Belt tabs (make 6)
Cast on 3 sts using 4mm (US 6) needles.
Work in rib as given for collar for 5 cm.
Cast off in rib.
Using photograph as a guide, stitch belt tabs in place around body, placing them 4 cm up from cast-on edge. Attach buckle to one end of belt, then thread belt through belt tabs.
All sizes
See information page for finishing instructions, setting in sleeves using the set-in method.

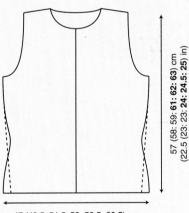

57 (58: 59: **61: 62: 63**) cm
(22.5 (23: 23: **24: 24.5: 25**) in)

47 (49.5: 51.5: **56: 58.5: 60.5**) cm
(18.5 (19.5: 20.5: **22: 23: 24**) in)

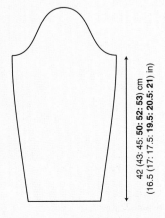

42 (43: 45: **50: 52: 53**) cm
(16.5 (17: 17.5: **19.5: 20.5: 21**) in)

Back cable chart

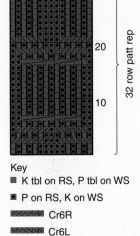

32
30

20

10

32 row patt rep

Right front cable chart

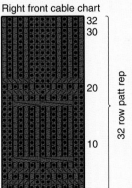
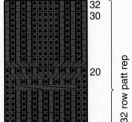

32
30

20

10

32 row patt rep

Key
▦ K tbl on RS, P tbl on WS
▨ P on RS, K on WS
▨ Cr6R
▨ Cr6L
▬ C11B
▬ C11F

65

HEPWORTH

LOUISA HARDING

YARN

		XS	S	M	L	XL
To fit bust		81	86	91	97	102cm
		32	34	36	38	40 in

Rowan Yorkshire Tweed DK

A Champion	346	7	8	8	8	9 x 50gm
B Frog	349	2	2	2	2	2 x 50gm
C Lime Leaf	348	1	1	1	1	1 x 50gm
D Revel	342	1	1	1	1	1 x 50gm
E Scarlet	344	1	1	1	1	1 x 50gm
F Frolic	350	1	1	1	1	1 x 50gm

NEEDLES

1 pair 3¼mm (no 10) (US 3) needles
1 pair 4mm (no 8) (US 6) needles

BUTTONS

7 x 75316

TENSION

20 sts and 28 rows to 10 cm measured over
stocking stitch using 4mm (US 6) needles.

BACK

Cast on 91 (95: 101: 105: 111) sts using 3¼mm
(US 3) needles and yarn A.
Row 1 (RS): K1 (1: 0: 0: 1), *P1, K1, rep from
* to last 0 (0: 1: 1: 0), P0 (0: 1: 1: 0).
Row 2: As row 1.
These 2 rows form moss st.
Work in moss st for a further 4 rows, ending
with a WS row.
Change to 4mm (US 6) needles.
Using the **intarsia** technique as described on
the information page, and starting and ending
rows as indicated, cont in patt from chart as folls:
Work 6 rows, ending with a WS row.
Dec 1 st at each end of next and every foll 6th
row until 79 (83: 89: 93: 99) sts rem.
Work 15 rows, ending with a WS row.
Inc 1 st at each end of next and every foll 6th
row until there are 91 (95: 101: 105: 111) sts,
taking inc sts into patt.
Cont straight until chart row 92 (96: 96: 98: 98)
has been completed, ending with a WS row.
(Work should measure 35 (36: 36: 37: 37) cm.)

Shape armholes

Keeping patt correct, cast off 3 (4: 4: 5: 5) sts at
beg of next 2 rows, then 3 sts at beg of foll 2 rows.
79 (81: 87: 89: 95) sts.
Dec 1 st at each end of next 3 (3: 5: 5: 7) rows,
then on foll 2 alt rows.
69 (71: 73: 75: 77) sts.
Cont straight until chart row 148 (152: 154: 158:
160) has been completed, ending with a WS row.
(Armhole should measure 20 (20: 21: 21: 22) cm.)

Shape shoulders and back neck

Cast off 7 (7: 7: 7: 8) sts at beg of next 2 rows.
55 (57: 59: 61: 61) sts.
Next row (RS): Cast off 7 (7: 7: 7: 8) sts, patt
until there are 11 (11: 12: 12: 11) sts on right
needle and turn, leaving rem sts on a holder.
Work each side of neck separately.
Cast off 4 sts at beg of next row.
Cast off rem 7 (7: 8: 8: 7) sts.
With RS facing, rejoin yarns to rem sts, cast off
centre 19 (21: 21: 23: 23) sts, patt to end.
Complete to match first side, reversing shapings.

LEFT FRONT

Cast on 51 (53: 56: 58: 61) sts using 3¼mm
(US 3) needles and yarn A.
Row 1 (RS): K1 (1: 0: 0: 1), *P1, K1, rep from
* to end.
Row 2: *K1, P1, rep from * to last 1 (1: 0: 0: 1) st,
K1 (1: 0: 0: 1).
These 2 rows form moss st.
Work in moss st for a further 3 rows, ending
with a RS row.
Row 6 (WS): Moss st 6 sts and slip these sts
onto a holder, M1, moss st to end.
46 (48: 51: 53: 56) sts.
Change to 4mm (US 6) needles.
Starting and ending rows as indicated, cont in
patt from chart as folls:
Work 6 rows, ending with a WS row.
Dec 1 st at beg of next and every foll 6th row
until 40 (42: 45: 47: 50) sts rem.
Work 15 rows, ending with a WS row.
Inc 1 st at beg of next and every foll 6th row
until there are 46 (48: 51: 53: 56) sts, taking inc
sts into patt.
Cont straight until left front matches back to
beg of armhole shaping, ending with a WS row.

Shape armhole and front slope

Keeping patt correct, cast off 3 (4: 4: 5: 5) sts at
beg and dec 1 st at end of next row.
42 (43: 46: 47: 50) sts.
Work 1 row.
Cast off 3 sts at beg and dec 1 st at end of next
row. 38 (39: 42: 43: 46) sts.
Work 1 row.
Dec 1 st at armhole edge of next 3 (3: 5: 5: 7) rows,
then on foll 2 alt rows **and at same time** dec 1 st
at front slope edge of next and foll 0 (2: 1: 3: 1)
alt rows, then on every foll 4th (0: 4th: 0: 4th) row.
31 (31: 32: 32: 33) sts.
Dec 1 st at front slope edge **only** on 2nd (2nd:
2nd: 2nd: 4th) and every foll 4th row until
21 (21: 22: 22: 23) sts rem.
Cont straight until left front matches back to
start of shoulder shaping, ending with a WS row.

Shape shoulder

Cast off 7 (7: 7: 7: 8) sts at beg of next and foll
alt row.
Work 1 row.
Cast off rem 7 (7: 8: 8: 7) sts.

RIGHT FRONT

Cast on 51 (53: 56: 58: 61) sts using 3¼mm
(US 3) needles and yarn A.

Row 1 (RS): *K1, P1, rep from * to last 1 (1:
0: 0: 1) st, K1 (1: 0: 0: 1).
Row 2: K1 (1: 0: 0: 1), *P1, K1, rep from * to
end.
These 2 rows form moss st.
Work in moss st for a further 2 rows, ending
with a WS row.
Row 5 (buttonhole row) (RS): K1, P1,
K2tog, yfwd, moss st to end.
Row 6: Moss st to last 6 sts, M1 and turn,
leaving last 6 sts on a holder. 46 (48: 51: 53: 56) sts.
Change to 4mm (US 6) needles.
Starting and ending rows as indicated, cont in
patt from chart as folls:
Work 6 rows, ending with a WS row.
Dec 1 st at end of next and every foll 6th row
until 40 (42: 45: 47: 50) sts rem.
Complete to match left front, reversing shapings.

SLEEVES (both alike)

Cast on 47 (47: 49: 51: 51) sts using 3¼mm
(US 3) needles and yarn A.
Row 1 (RS): K1 (1: 0: 1: 1), *P1, K1, rep from
* to last 0 (0: 1: 0: 0) st, P0 (0: 1: 0: 0).
Row 2: As row 1.
These 2 rows form moss st.
Work in moss st for a further 4 rows, ending
with a WS row.
Change to 4mm (US 6) needles.
Starting and ending rows as indicated, cont in
patt from chart, shaping sides by inc 1 st at each
end of 7th and every foll 14th (12th: 14th: 14th:
12th) row to 61 (67: 55: 57: 65) sts, then on
every foll 12th (-: 12th: 12th: 10th) row until
there are 65 (-: 69: 71: 73) sts, taking inc sts into
patt.
Cont straight until sleeve measures 48 (48: 49:
49: 49) cm, ending with a WS row.

Shape top

Keeping patt correct, cast off 3 (4: 4: 5: 5) sts at
beg of next 2 rows. 59 (59: 61: 61: 63) sts.
Dec 1 st at each end of next 3 rows, then on
foll 5 alt rows, then on every foll 4th row until
37 (37: 39: 39: 41) sts rem.
Work 1 row.
Dec 1 st at each end of next and every foll alt
row until 29 sts rem, then on foll row, ending
with a WS row. 27 sts.
Cast off 3 sts at beg of next 4 rows.
Cast off rem 15 sts.

MAKING UP

PRESS as described on the information page.
Join both shoulder seams using back stitch, or
mattress st if preferred.
Place markers along front slope edges 12 cm
down from shoulder seams.

Button band and left collar

Slip 6 sts from left front holder onto 3¼mm
(US 3) needles and rejoin yarn A with RS
facing.
Cont in moss st as set until band, when slightly
stretched, fits up left front opening edge to start
of front slope shaping, ending with a **RS** row.
Slip stitch band in place.

Shape for collar

Next row (RS of collar, WS of front): K1,
P into front, back and front again of next st,
moss st to end. 8 sts.
Work 3 rows.
Rep last 4 rows 9 times more, then first of these
rows again. 28 sts.
Cont straight until collar, unstretched, fits up
front slope to marker, ending at free (outer)
edge.

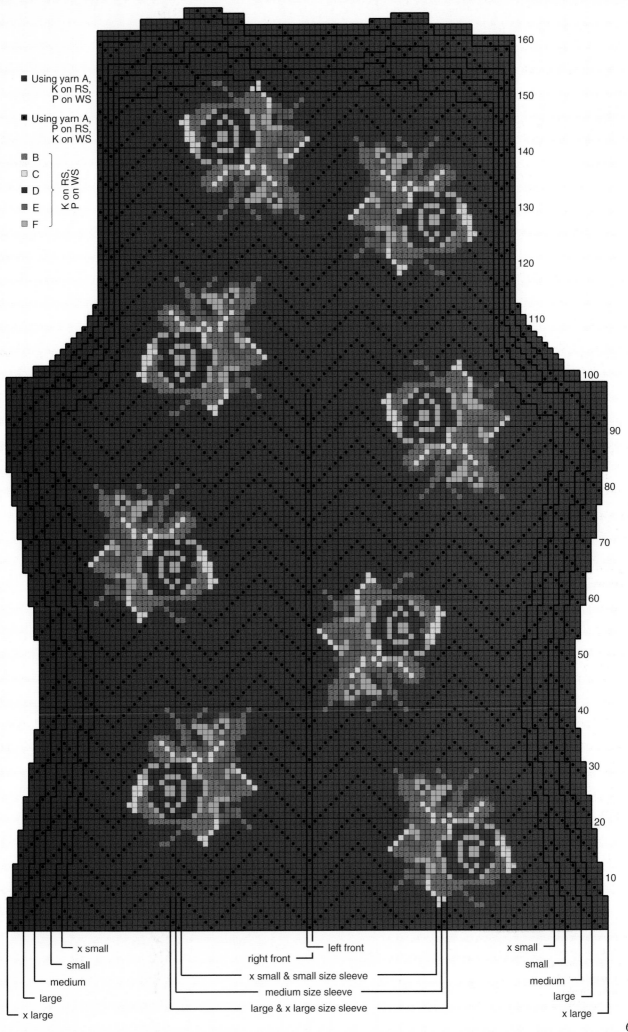

Using yarn A,
K on RS,
P on WS

Using yarn A,
P on RS,
K on WS

B
C
D
E
F

K on RS,
P on WS

160
150
140
130
120
110
100
90
80
70
60
50
40
30
20
10

x small
small
medium
large
x large

right front
left front
x small & small size sleeve
medium size sleeve
large & x large size sleeve

x small
small
medium
large
x large

Next row: Cast off 11 sts, turn and cast on 11 sts, moss st to end.

Cont straight until collar, unstretched, fits up front slope and across to centre back neck. Cast off.

Mark positions for 7 buttons on this band – first to come level with buttonhole already worked in right front, last to come 1 cm below start of front slope shaping and rem 5 evenly spaced between.

Buttonhole band and right collar

Slip 6 sts from right front holder onto 3¼mm (US 3) needles and rejoin yarn A with WS facing.

Cont in moss st as set until band, when slightly stretched, fits up right front opening edge to start of front slope shaping, ending with a **RS** row and with the addition of a further 6 buttonholes worked to correspond with positions marked for buttons as folls:

Buttonhole row (RS): K1, P1, K2tog, yfwd, K1, P1.

Slip stitch band in place.

Shape for collar

Next row (RS of collar, WS of front): Moss st to last 2 sts, P into front, back and front again of next st, K1. 8 sts.

Complete to match left collar, reversing shapings.

Join centre back seam of collar, then sew collar in place to front slope and back neck edges.

See information page for finishing instructions, setting in sleeves using the set-in method.

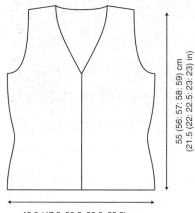

45.5 (47.5: 50.5: 52.5: 55.5) cm
(18 (18.5: 20: 20.5: 22) in)

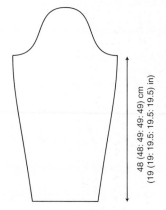

HOME SWEET HOME

KIM HARGREAVES

YARN

		XS	S	M	L	XL	
To fit bust		81	86	91	97	102	cm
		32	34	36	38	40	in
Rowan Magpie							
A Charcoal	625	2	2	2	3	3	x 100gm
B Boggy	690	6	7	7	7	8	x 100gm
C Toad	694	1	1	1	1	1	x 100gm
D Morning Dew	692	1	1	1	1	1	x 100gm
E Gurgle	695	1	1	1	1	1	x 100gm
F Misty	318	1	1	1	1	1	x 100gm
G Float	691	1	1	1	1	1	x 100gm
H Prance	667	1	1	1	1	1	x 100gm
J Truffle	320	1	1	1	1	1	x 100gm
L Tranquil	689	1	1	1	1	1	x 100gm

NEEDLES

1 pair 4mm (no 8) (US 6) needles
1 pair 5mm (no 6) (US 8) needles

TENSION

18 sts and 23 rows to 10 cm measured over stocking stitch using 5mm (US 8) needles.

BACK

Cast on 106 (110: 114: 118: 122) sts using 4mm (US 6) needles and yarn A.

Row 1 (RS): K2, *P2, K2, rep from * to end.
Row 2: P2, *K2, P2, rep from * to end.
These 2 rows form rib.

Work in rib for a further 6 rows, dec 1 st at end of last row and ending with a WS row.
105 (109: 113: 117: 121) sts.

Change to 5mm (US 8) needles.

Using the **intarsia** technique as described on the information page and starting and ending rows as indicated, cont in patt from chart for border, which is worked entirely in st st beg with a K row, until all 54 rows have been completed.

Break off contrasts and cont in st st using yarn B **only.★★**

Cont straight until back measures 45 (46: 46: 47: 47) cm, ending with a WS row.

Shape armholes

Cast off 5 sts at beg of next 2 rows.
95 (99: 103: 107: 111) sts.

Cont straight until armhole measures 25 (25: 26: 26: 27) cm, ending with a WS row.

Shape shoulders and back neck

Cast off 10 (11: 11: 12: 12) sts at beg of next 2 rows.
75 (77: 81: 83: 87) sts.

Next row (RS): Cast off 10 (11: 11: 12: 12) sts, K until there are 15 (16: 16: 15: 17) sts on right needle and turn, leaving rem sts on a holder.

Work each side of neck separately.
Cast off 4 sts at beg of next row.
Cast off rem 11 (10: 12: 11: 13) sts.
With RS facing, rejoin yarn to rem sts, cast off centre 25 (27: 27: 29: 29) sts, K to end.
Complete to match first side, reversing shapings.

FRONT

Work as given for back to ★★.

Cont straight until front measures 37 (38: 38: 39: 39) cm, ending with a WS row.

Place chart

Using the **intarsia** technique as described on the information page, cont as folls:

Next row (RS): K8 (10: 12: 14: 16), work next 89 sts as row 1 of chart for front, K to end.

Next row: P8 (10: 12: 14: 16), work next 89 sts as row 2 of chart for front, P to end.

These 2 rows set the sts - centre 89 sts foll chart for front and side sts in st st using yarn B.

Cont straight until left front matches back to beg of armhole shaping, ending with a WS row.

Shape armholes

Keeping chart correct, cast off 5 sts at beg of next 2 rows. 95 (99: 103: 107: 111) sts.

Cont straight until all 48 rows of chart have been completed, ending with a WS row.

Break off contrasts and cont in st st using yarn B **only**.

Cont straight until 14 (14: 14: 16: 16) rows less have been worked than on back to start of shoulder shaping, ending with a WS row.

Shape neck

Next row (RS): K39 (40: 42: 44: 46) and turn, leaving rem sts on a holder.

Work each side of neck separately.
Dec 1 st at neck edge of next 6 rows, then on foll 2 (2: 2: 3: 3) alt rows. 31 (32: 34: 35: 37) sts.
Work 3 rows, ending with a WS row.

Shape shoulder

Cast off 10 (11: 11: 12: 12) sts at beg of next and foll alt row.
Work 1 row.
Cast off rem 11 (10: 12: 11: 13) sts.
With RS facing, rejoin yarn to rem sts, cast off centre 17 (19: 19: 19: 19) sts, K to end.
Complete to match first side, reversing shapings.

SLEEVES (both alike)

Cast on 54 (54: 58: 58: 58) sts using 4mm (US 6) needles and yarn A.

Work in rib as given for back for 8 rows, inc (inc: dec: inc: inc) 1 st at end of last row and ending with a WS row. 55 (55: 57: 59: 59) sts.
Change to 5mm (US 8) needles.

Starting and ending rows as indicated, cont in patt from chart for border until chart row 34 has been completed, ending with a WS row,

and at same time inc 1 st at each end of 3rd and every foll 8th row to 61 (61: 63: 65: 65) sts, then on every foll 6th row. 65 (65: 67: 69: 69) sts.
Break off contrasts and cont in st st using yarn B **only**.

Inc 1 st at each end of next (next: 3rd: 3rd: 3rd) and every foll 4th (4th: 4th: 6th: 4th) row to 91 (91: 93: 75: 95) sts, then on every foll - (-: -: 4th: -) row until there are - (-: -: 93: -) sts.

Cont straight until sleeve measures 46 (46: 47: 47: 47) cm, ending with a WS row.
Cast off.

MAKING UP

PRESS as described on the information page.
Join right shoulder seam using back stitch, or mattress st if preferred.

Neckband

With RS facing, using 4mm (US 6) needles and yarn B, pick up and knit 18 (18: 18: 19: 19) sts down left side of neck, 17 (19: 19: 19: 19) sts from front, 18 (18: 18: 19: 19) sts up right side of neck, then 33 (35: 35: 37: 37) sts from back.
86 (90: 90: 94: 94) sts.
Work in rib as given for back for 8 rows.
Cast off in rib.
See information page for finishing instructions, setting in sleeves using the square set-in method.

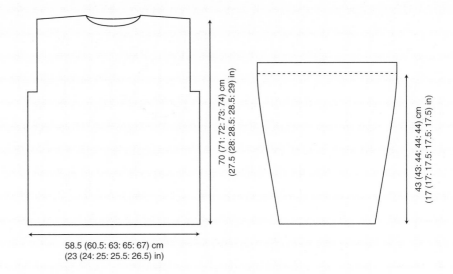

70 (71: 72: 73: 74) cm
(27.5 (28: 28.5: 28.5: 29) in)

43 (43: 44: 44: 44) cm
(17 (17: 17.5: 17.5: 17.5) in)

58.5 (60.5: 63: 65: 67) cm
(23 (24: 25: 25.5: 26.5) in)

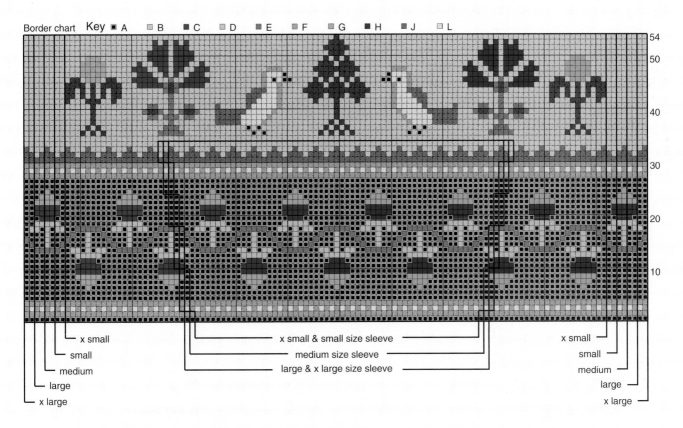

Border chart Key ■ A □ B ■ C □ D ■ E □ F □ G ■ H ■ J □ L

x small
small
medium
large
x large

x small & small size sleeve
medium size sleeve
large & x large size sleeve

x small
small
medium
large
x large

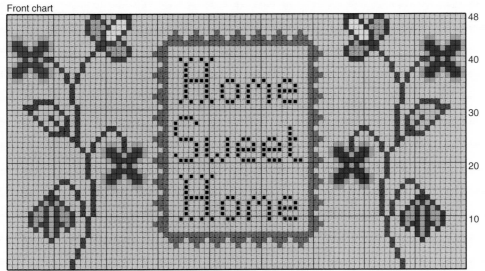

Front chart

Design number 15

STOCKSMOOR

LOUISA HARDING

YARN

	S	M	L	XL	XXL	
To fit chest	97	102	107	112	117	cm
	38	40	42	44	46	in

Rowan Yorkshire Tweed Chunky

A Stout	5	5	4	6	6	6	7	7	x 100gm
B String	5	5	1	5	5	5	6	6	x 100gm

NEEDLES

1 pair 7mm (no 2) (US 10½) needles
1 pair 8mm (no 0) (US 11) needles
Cable needle

TENSION

12 sts and 16 rows to 10 cm measured over stocking stitch using 8mm (US 11) needles.

SPECIAL ABBREVIATIONS

Cr3L = Cross 3 left Slip next 2 sts onto cn and leave at front of work, P1, then K2 from cn
Cr3R = Cross 3 right Slip next st onto cn and leave at back of work, K2, then P1 from cn
C4F = Cable 4 front Slip next 2 sts onto cn and leave at front of work, K2, then K2 from cn

BACK

Cast on 80 (84: 86: 90: 92) sts using 7mm (US 10½) needles and yarn A.
Row 1 (RS): K3 (5: 6: 0: 1), P2, *K6, P2, rep from * to last 3 (5: 6: 0: 1) sts, K3 (5: 6: 0: 1).
Row 2: P3 (5: 6: 0: 1), K2, *P6, K2, rep from * to last 3 (5: 6: 0: 1) sts, P3 (5: 6: 0: 1).
These 2 rows form rib.
Work in rib for a further 9 rows, ending with a RS row.
Row 12 (WS): Rib 23 (25: 26: 28: 29), (M1, rib 2, M1, rib 14) twice, M1, rib 2, M1, rib to end. 86 (90: 92: 96: 98) sts.
Change to 8mm (US 11) needles.
Join in yarn B.
Cont in striped cable patt as folls:
Row 1 (RS): Using yarn B, K19 (21: 22: 24: 25), (P2, K2, P4, K2, P2, K6) twice, P2, K2, P4, K2, P2, K to end.
Row 2: Using yarn B, P19 (21: 22: 24: 25), (K2, P2, K4, P2, K2, P6) twice, K2, P2, K4, P2, K2, P to end.

Row 3: Using yarn B, K19 (21: 22: 24: 25), (P2, Cr3L, P2, Cr3R, P2, K6) twice, P2, Cr3L, P2, Cr3R, P2, K to end.
Row 4: Using yarn B, P19 (21: 22: 24: 25), (K3, P2, K2, P2, K3, P6) twice, K3, P2, K2, P2, K3, P to end.
Row 5: Using yarn B, K19 (21: 22: 24: 25), (P3, Cr3L, Cr3R, P3, K6) twice, P3, Cr3L, Cr3R, P3, K to end.
Row 6: Using yarn B, P19 (21: 22: 24: 25), (K4, P4, K4, P6) twice, K4, P4, K4, P to end.
Row 7: Using yarn B, K19 (21: 22: 24: 25), (P4, C4F, P4, K6) twice, P4, C4F, P4, K to end.
Row 8: As row 6.
Row 9: Using yarn B, K19 (21: 22: 24: 25), (P3, Cr3R, Cr3L, P3, K6) twice, P3, Cr3R, Cr3L, P3, K to end.
Row 10: As row 4.
Row 11: Using yarn B, K19 (21: 22: 24: 25), (P2, Cr3R, P2, Cr3L, P2, K6) twice, P2, Cr3R, P2, Cr3L, P2, K to end.
Row 12: As row 2.
Rows 13 to 24: As rows 1 to 12 but using yarn A.
These 24 rows form patt.
Cont in patt until back measures 45 (45: 46: 46: 47) cm, ending with a WS row.
Shape armholes
Keeping patt correct, cast off 6 sts at beg of next 2 rows. 74 (78: 80: 84: 86) sts.
Cont straight until armhole measures 24 (25: 25: 26: 26) cm, ending with a WS row.
Shape shoulders and back neck
Cast off 8 (9: 9: 9: 9) sts at beg of next 2 rows. 58 (60: 62: 66: 68) sts.
Next row (RS): Cast off 8 (9: 9: 9: 9) sts, patt until there are 13 (12: 13: 14: 14) sts on right needle and turn, leaving rem sts on a holder.
Work each side of neck separately.
Cast off 4 sts at beg of next row.
Cast off rem 9 (8: 9: 10: 10) sts.
With RS facing, rejoin yarns to rem sts, cast off centre 16 (18: 18: 20: 22) sts, patt to end.
Complete to match first side, reversing shapings.

FRONT

Work as given for back until 8 (8: 10: 10: 10) rows less have been worked than on back to start of shoulder shaping, ending with a WS row.
Shape neck
Next row (RS): Patt 33 (34: 36: 37: 37) sts and turn, leaving rem sts on a holder.
Work each side of neck separately.

Cast off 4 sts at beg of next row.
29 (30: 32: 33: 33) sts.
Dec 1 st at neck edge of next 4 rows, then on foll 0 (0: 1: 1: 1) alt row.
25 (26: 27: 28: 28) sts.
Work 2 rows, ending with a WS row.
Shape shoulder
Cast off 8 (9: 9: 9: 9) sts at beg of next and foll alt row.
Work 1 row.
Cast off rem 9 (8: 9: 10: 10) sts.
With RS facing, rejoin yarns to rem sts, cast off centre 8 (10: 8: 10: 12) sts, patt to end.
Complete to match first side, reversing shapings.

SLEEVES (both alike)

Cast on 38 (38: 40: 40: 40) sts using 7mm (US 10½) needles and yarn A.
Row 1 (RS): P0 (0: 1: 1: 1), K6, *P2, K6, rep from * to last 0 (0: 1: 1: 1) sts, P0 (0: 1: 1: 1).
Row 2: K0 (0: 1: 1: 1), P6, *K2, P6, rep from * to last 0 (0: 1: 1: 1) sts, K0 (0: 1: 1: 1).
These 2 rows form rib.
Work in rib for a further 9 rows, ending with a RS row.
Row 12 (WS): Rib 18 (18: 19: 19: 19), M1, rib 2, M1, rib to end.
40 (40: 42: 42: 42) sts.
Change to 8mm (US 11) needles.
Join in yarn B.
Cont in striped cable patt as folls:
Row 1 (RS): Using yarn B, inc in first st, K13 (13: 14: 14: 14), P2, K2, P4, K2, P2, K to last st, inc in last st. 42 (42: 44: 44: 44) sts.
Row 2: Using yarn B, P15 (15: 16: 16: 16), K2, P2, K4, P2, K2, P to end.
Row 3: Using yarn B, K15 (15: 16: 16: 16), P2, Cr3L, P2, Cr3R, P2, K to end.
Row 4: Using yarn B, P15 (15: 16: 16: 16), K3, P2, K2, P2, K3, P to end.
Row 5: Using yarn B, K15 (15: 16: 16: 16), P3, Cr3L, Cr3R, P3, K to end.
Row 6: Using yarn B, P15 (15: 16: 16: 16), K4, P4, K4, P to end.
Row 7: Using yarn B, inc in first st, K14 (14: 15: 15: 15), P4, C4F, P4, K to last st, inc in last st. 44 (44: 46: 46: 46) sts.
Row 8: Using yarn B, P16 (16: 17: 17: 17), K4, P4, K4, P to end.
Row 9: Using yarn B, K16 (16: 17: 17: 17), P3, Cr3R, Cr3L, P3, K to end.
Row 10: Using yarn B, P16 (16: 17: 17: 17), K3, P2, K2, P2, K3, P to end.

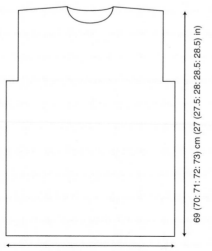

66.5 (70: 71.5: 75: 76.5) cm
(26 (27.5: 28: 29.5: 30) in)

69 (70: 71: 72: 73) cm (27 (27.5: 28: 28.5: 28.5) in)

44 (45: 45: 46: 46) cm (17.5 (17.5: 17.5: 18: 18) in)

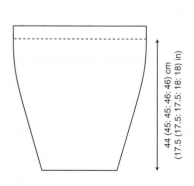

Row 11: Using yarn B, K16 (16: 17: 17: 17), P2, Cr3R, P2, Cr3L, P2, K to end.
Row 12: Using yarn B, P16 (16: 17: 17: 17), K2, P2, K4, P2, K2, P to end.
These 12 rows set position of patt as given for back. Beg with 12 rows using yarn A, cont in patt, shaping sides by inc 1 st at each end of next and every foll 6th row to 56 (54: 60: 58: 58) sts, then on every foll 4th row until there are 60 (62: 62: 64: 64) sts, taking inc sts into st st.

Cont straight until sleeve measures 49 (50: 50: 51: 51) cm, ending with a WS row. Cast off.

MAKING UP
PRESS as described on the information page. Join right shoulder seam using back stitch, or mattress st if preferred.
Neckband
With RS facing, using 7mm (US 10½) needles and yarn A, pick up and knit 14 (15: 16: 15: 16) sts down left side of neck, 8 (10: 8: 10: 12) sts from front, 14 (15: 16: 15: 16) sts up right side of neck, then 22 (26: 26: 26: 30) sts from back.
58 (66: 66: 66: 74) sts.
Row 1 (WS): K2, *P6, K2, rep from * to end.
Row 2: P2, *K6, P2, rep from * to end.
Rep these 2 rows until neckband measures 7 cm. Cast off in rib.
See information page for finishing instructions, setting in sleeves using the square set-in method.

Design number 16

KIRKBY

MARTIN STOREY

YARN

	ladies			mens		
	S	M	L	M	L	XL
To fit bust/chest	86	91	97	102	107	112 cm
	34	36	38	40	42	44 in

Rowan Yorkshire Tweed Aran

7	7	8	9	10	10 x 100gm

(ladies photographed in Bramble 416, mans in Thorny 412)

NEEDLES
1 pair 4mm (no 8) (US 6) needles
1 pair 5mm (no 6) (US 8) needles
Cable needle

TENSION
16 sts and 23 rows to 10 cm measured over stocking stitch using 5mm (US 8) needles.

SPECIAL ABBREVIATIONS
C4B = Cable 4 back Slip next 2 sts onto cable needle and leave at back of work, K2, then K2 from cable needle
C4F = Cable 4 front Slip next 2 sts onto cable needle and leave at front of work, K2, then K2 from cable needle
Cr4R = Cross 4 right Slip next st onto cable needle and leave at back of work, K3, then P (or K depending on point in patt) st from cable needle
Cr4L = Cross 4 left Slip next 3 sts onto cable needle and leave at front of work, P (or K depending on point in patt) 1 st, then K3 from cable needle
C7B = Cable 7 back Slip next 4 sts onto cable needle and leave at back of work, K3, then K4 from cable needle
MB = Make bobble (K1, yfwd, K1, yfwd, K1) all into next st, turn, P5, turn, K5, turn, P2tog, K1, P2tog, turn, sl 1, K2tog, psso

Pattern note: The pattern is written for the 3 ladies sizes, followed by the mens sizes in **bold**. Where only one figure appears this applies to all sizes in that group.

BACK
Cast on 75 (79: 83: **93: 97: 101**) sts using 4mm (US 6) needles.
Row 1 (RS): K0 (2: 0: **0: 0: 1**), P3 (3: 1: **0: 2: 3**), *K3, P3, rep from * to last 0 (2: 4: **3: 5: 1**) sts, K0 (2: 3: **3: 3: 1**), P0 (0: 1: **0: 2: 0**).
Row 2: P0 (2: 0: **0: 0: 1**), K3 (3: 1: **0: 2: 3**), *P3, K3, rep from * to last 0 (2: 4: **3: 5: 1**) sts, P0 (2: 3: **3: 3: 1**), K0 (0: 1: **0: 2: 0**).
These 2 rows form rib.
Work in rib for a further 15 rows, ending with a RS row.
Row 18 (WS): Rib 22 (24: 26: **18: 20: 22**), *(M1, rib 1) 5 times, M1, rib 10, (M1, rib 1) twice, M1, rib 9, rep from * 0 (**1**) times more, (M1, rib 1) 5 times, M1, rib to end.
90 (94: 98: **117: 121: 125**) sts.
Change to 5mm (US 8) needles.
Cont in patt as folls:
Row 1 (RS): (K1, P1) 7 (8: 9: **5: 6: 7**) times, *work next 27 sts as row 1 of cable chart, P1, C4B, K2, P1, rep from * 0 (**1**) times more, work next 27 sts as row 1 of cable chart, (P1, K1) to end.

Row 2: (K1, P1) 7 (8: 9: **5: 6: 7**) times, *work next 27 sts as row 2 of cable chart, K1, P6, K1, rep from * 0 (**1**) times more, work next 27 sts as row 2 of cable chart, (P1, K1) to end.
Row 3: (K1, P1) 7 (8: 9: **5: 6: 7**) times, *work next 27 sts as row 1 of cable chart, P1, K2, C4F, P1, rep from * 0 (**1**) times more, work next 27 sts as row 1 of cable chart, (P1, K1) to end.
Row 4: As row 2.
These 4 rows set the sts – 2 (**3**) cable panels separated by cables and moss st at sides.
Keeping sts correct as set, cont as folls:
Ladies sizes only
Dec 1 st at each end of 7th and foll 6th row, then on foll 4th row. 84 (88: 92) sts.
Work 9 rows.
Inc 1 st at each end of next and every foll 14th row until there are 90 (94: 98) sts, taking inc sts into moss st.
All sizes
Cont straight until back measures 38 (39: 40: **45: 46: 47**) cm, ending with a WS row.
Shape armholes
Keeping patt correct, cast off 5 (6: 7: **5: 6: 7**) sts at beg of next 2 rows.
80 (82: 84: **107: 109: 111**) sts.
Dec 1 st at each end of next 3 rows, then on foll 1 (**2**) alt rows, then on foll 4th row.
70 (72: 74: **95: 97: 99**) sts.
Cont straight until armhole measures 20 (21: 22: **23: 24: 25**) cm, ending with a WS row.
Shape shoulders and back neck
Cast off 6 (**11**) sts at beg of next 2 rows.
58 (60: 62: **73: 75: 77**) sts.

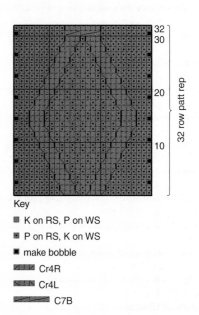

32
30
20
10
32 row patt rep

Key
■ K on RS, P on WS
■ P on RS, K on WS
■ make bobble
⊠ Cr4R
⊠ Cr4L
⊠ C7B

Next row (RS): Cast off 6 (**11**) sts, patt until there are 11 (**14**) sts on right needle and turn, leaving rem sts on a holder.
Work each side of neck separately.
Cast off 4 sts at beg of next row.
Cast off rem 7 (**10**) sts.
With RS facing, rejoin yarn to rem sts, cast off centre 24 (26: 28: **23: 25: 27**) sts dec 6 sts evenly, patt to end.
Complete to match first side, reversing shapings.

FRONT

Work as given for back until 12 rows less have been worked than on back to start of shoulder shaping, ending with a WS row.

Shape neck
Next row (RS): Patt 27 (**39**) sts and turn, leaving rem sts on a holder.
Work each side of neck separately.
Dec 1 st at neck edge of next 5 (**3**) rows, then on foll 3 (**4**) alt rows, ending with a WS row.
19 (**32**) sts.

Shape shoulder
Cast off 6 (**11**) sts at beg of next and foll alt row.
Work 1 row.
Cast off rem 7 (**10**) sts.
With RS facing, rejoin yarn to rem sts, cast off centre 16 (18: 20: **17: 19: 21**) sts dec 6 sts evenly, patt to end.
Complete to match first side, reversing shapings.

SLEEVES (both alike)

Cast on 35 (37: 39: **39: 41: 43**) sts using 4mm (US 6) needles.
Row 1 (RS): K0 (0: 1: **2**), P1 (2: 3: **3**), *K3, P3, rep from * to last 4 (5: 0: **0: 1: 2**) sts, K3 (3: 0: **0: 1: 2**), P1 (2: 0: **0**).
Row 2: P0 (**0: 1: 2**), K1 (2: 3: **3**), *P3, K3, rep from * to last 4 (5: 0: **0: 1: 2**) sts, P3 (3: 0: **0: 1: 2**), K1 (2: 0: **0**).
These 2 rows form rib.
Work in rib for a further 15 rows, ending with a RS row.
Row 18 (WS): Rib 15 (16: 17: **17: 18: 19**), (M1, rib 1) 5 times, M1, rib to end.
41 (43: 45: **45: 47: 49**) sts.
Change to 5mm (US 8) needles.
Cont in patt as folls:
Row 1 (RS): Inc in first st, P0 (1: 0: **0: 1: 0**), (K1, P1) 3 (3: 4: **4: 4: 5**) times, work next 27 sts as row 1 of cable chart, (P1, K1) 3 (3: 4: **4: 4: 5**) times, P0 (1: 0: **0: 1: 0**), inc in last st.
43 (45: 47: **47: 49: 51**) sts.
Row 2: P0 (1: 0: **0: 1: 0**), (K1, P1) 4 (4: 5: **5: 5: 6**) times, work next 27 sts as row 2 of cable chart, (P1, K1) 4 (4: 5: **5: 5: 6**) times, P0 (1: 0: **0: 1: 0**).
These 2 rows set the sts – cable panel with moss st at sides.
Keeping sts correct as set, cont as folls:
Inc 1 st at each end of 9th (**7th**) and every foll 10th (**8th**) row to 47 (49: 53: **55: 61: 65**) sts, then on every foll 8th (**6th**) row until there are 61 (63: 65: **71: 73: 75**) sts, taking inc sts into moss st.
Cont straight until sleeve measures 45 (46: 47: **48: 49: 50**) cm, ending with a WS row.

Shape top
Keeping patt correct, cast off 5 (6: 7: **5: 6: 7**) sts at beg of next 2 rows. 51 (**61**) sts.
Dec 1 st at each end of next 3 rows, then on foll alt row, then on every foll 4th row until 35 (**45**) sts rem.
Work 1 row, ending with a WS row.
Dec 1 st at each end of next and foll 3 alt rows, then on foll 3 rows, ending with a WS row.
21 (**31**) sts.

Mens sizes only
Cast off 5 sts at beg of next 2 rows. 21 sts.
All sizes
Cast off rem 21 sts.

MAKING UP

PRESS as described on the information page.
Join right shoulder seam using back stitch, or mattress st if preferred.
Collar
With RS facing and using 4mm (US 6) needles, pick up and knit 14 (**16**) sts down left side of neck, 12 (15: 15: **12: 15: 15**) sts from front, 14 (**16**) sts up right side of neck, then 26 (29: 29: **28: 31: 31**) sts from back.
66 (72: 72: **72: 78: 78**) sts.
Row 1 (WS): *P3, K3, rep from * to end.
Rep this row until collar measures 5 cm.
Change to 5mm (US 8) needles.
Cont in rib until collar measures 16 cm.
Cast off in rib.
See information page for finishing instructions, setting in sleeves using the set-in method and reversing collar seam for turn-back.

BILBERRY

LOUISA HARDING

YARN

	XS	S	M	L	XL		
To fit bust	81	86	91	97	102	cm	
	32	34	36	38	40	in	
Rowan Yorkshire Tweed DK							
A Revel	342 8	9	9	10	10	x	50gm
B Frog	349 1	1	1	2	2	x	50gm
C Scarlet	344 1	1	1	1	1	x	50gm
D Frolic	350 1	1	1	1	1	x	50gm

NEEDLES

1 pair 3¼mm (no 10) (US 3) needles
1 pair 4mm (no 8) (US 6) needles
Cable needle

TENSION

20 sts and 28 rows to 10 cm measured over stocking stitch using 4mm (US 6) needles.

SPECIAL ABBREVIATIONS

Cr3L = Cross 3 left Slip next 2 sts onto cable needle and leave at front of work, P1, then K2 from cable needle
Cr3R = Cross 3 right Slip next st onto cable needle and leave at back of work, K2, then P1 from cable needle
C4F = Cable 4 front Slip next 2 sts onto cable needle and leave at front of work, K2, then K2 from cable needle
C4B = Cable 4 back Slip next 2 sts onto cable needle and leave at back of work, K2, then K2 from cable needle

BACK and FRONT (both alike)

Cast on 106 (112: 116: 122: 126) sts using 3¼mm (US 3) needles and yarn A.
Row 1 (RS): K1 (0: 0: 3: 0), P2 (0: 2: 2: 1), *K4, P2, rep from * to last 1 (4: 0: 3: 5) sts, K1 (4: 0: 3: 4), P0 (0: 0: 0: 1).
Row 2: P1 (0: 0: 3: 0), K2 (0: 2: 2: 1), *P4, K2, rep from * to last 1 (4: 0: 3: 5) sts, P1 (4: 0: 3: 4), K0 (0: 0: 0: 1).
These 2 rows form rib.
Work in rib for a further 11 rows, ending with a RS row.
Row 14 (WS): Rib 28 (31: 33: 36: 38), (M1,

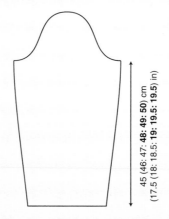

47 (49.5: 52: **58: 60.5: 63**) cm
(18.5 (19.5: 20.5: **23: 24: 25**) in)

58 (60: 62: **68: 70: 72**) cm
(23 (23.5: 24.5: **27: 27.5: 28.5**) in)

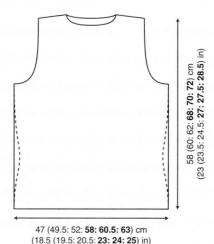

45 (46: 47: **48: 49: 50**) cm
(17.5 (18: 18.5: **19: 19.5: 19.5**) in)

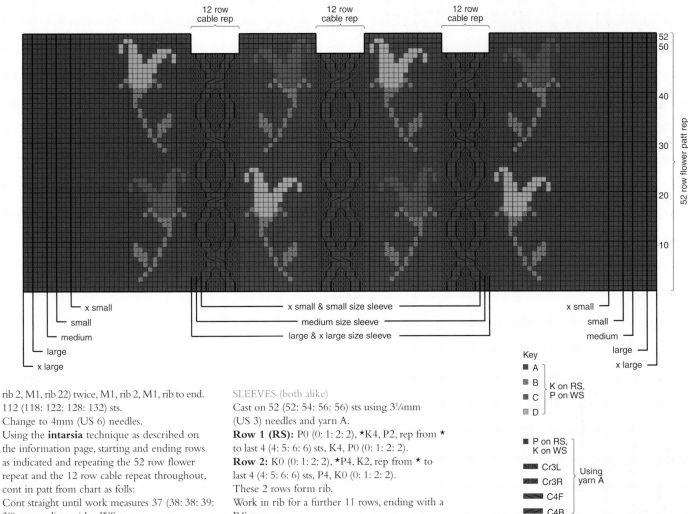

12 row cable rep   12 row cable rep   12 row cable rep

52 row flower patt rep

52 / 50 / 40 / 30 / 20 / 10

x small / small / medium / large / x large

x small & small size sleeve / medium size sleeve / large & x large size sleeve

x small / small / medium / large / x large

Key
- ■ A
- ■ B
- ■ C   } K on RS, P on WS
- □ D

- ■ P on RS, K on WS

- ▨ Cr3L
- ▨ Cr3R   } Using
- ▨ C4F   yarn A
- ▨ C4B

rib 2, M1, rib 22) twice, M1, rib 2, M1, rib to end.
112 (118: 122: 128: 132) sts.
Change to 4mm (US 6) needles.
Using the **intarsia** technique as described on
the information page, starting and ending rows
as indicated and repeating the 52 row flower
repeat and the 12 row cable repeat throughout,
cont in patt from chart as folls:
Cont straight until work measures 37 (38: 38: 39:
39) cm, ending with a WS row.
Shape armholes
Keeping patt correct, cast off 5 (6: 6: 7: 7) sts at
beg of next 2 rows. 102 (106: 110: 114: 118) sts.
Dec 1 st at each end of next 3 (3: 5: 5: 7) rows,
then on foll 1 (2: 1: 2: 1) alt rows, then on every
foll 4th row until 90 (92: 94: 96: 98) sts rem.
Cont straight until armhole measures approx
15 (14: 14: 13: 13) cm, ending after chart row 28
and with a WS row.
Change to 3¼mm (US 3) needles.
Break off all contrasts and cont using yarn A only.
Next row (RS): P0 (0: 0: 1: 2), K2 (3: 4: 4: 4),
(P2, K4) twice, *P2, K2tog, K2, K2tog tbl, (P2, K4)
3 times, rep from * once more, P2, K2tog, K2,
K2tog tbl, P2, (K4, P2) twice, K2 (3: 4: 4: 4),
P0 (0: 0: 1: 2). 84 (86: 88: 90: 92) sts.
Next row: K0 (0: 0: 1: 0), P2 (3: 4: 4: 0), *K2, P4,
rep from * to last 4 (5: 0: 1: 2) sts, K2 (2: 0: 1: 2),
P2 (3: 0: 0: 0).
Next row: P0 (0: 0: 1: 0), K2 (3: 4: 4: 0), *P2, K4,
rep from * to last 4 (5: 0: 1: 2) sts, P2 (2: 0: 1: 2),
K2 (3: 0: 0: 0).
Last 2 rows form rib.
Cont in rib until armholes measure 19 (19: 20:
20: 21) cm, ending with a WS row.
Shape neck and shoulders
Next row (RS): Rib 32 (32: 33: 33: 34) and
turn, leaving rem sts on a holder.
Work each side of neck separately.
Cast off 4 sts at beg of next row, and 7 sts at beg
of foll row.
Rep last 2 rows once more. 10 (10: 11: 11: 12) sts.
Cast off 4 sts at beg of next row.
Cast off rem 6 (6: 7: 7: 8) sts.
With RS facing, rejoin yarn to rem sts, cast off
centre 20 (22: 22: 24: 24) sts, rib to end.
Complete to match first side, reversing shapings.

SLEEVES (both alike)
Cast on 52 (52: 54: 56: 56) sts using 3¼mm
(US 3) needles and yarn A.
Row 1 (RS): P0 (0: 1: 2: 2), *K4, P2, rep from *
to last 4 (4: 5: 6: 6) sts, K4, P0 (0: 1: 2: 2).
Row 2: K0 (0: 1: 2: 2), *P4, K2, rep from * to
last 4 (4: 5: 6: 6) sts, P4, K0 (0: 1: 2: 2).
These 2 rows form rib.
Work in rib for a further 11 rows, ending with a
RS row.
Row 14 (WS): Rib 1 (1: 2: 3: 3), (M1, rib 2,
M1, rib 22) twice, M1, rib 2, M1, rib to end.
58 (58: 60: 62: 62) sts.
Change to 4mm (US 6) needles.
Starting and ending rows as indicated, cont in
patt from chart, shaping sides by inc 1 st at each
end of 3rd and every foll 14th (12th: 12th: 12th:
10th) row to 70 (70: 68: 70: 66) sts, then on
every foll 16th (14th: 14th: 14th: 12th) row until
there are 72 (74: 76: 78: 80) sts, taking inc sts
beyond cables into st st.
Cont straight until sleeve measures 41 (41: 42:
42: 42) cm, ending with a WS row.
Shape top
Keeping patt correct, cast off 5 (6: 6: 7: 7) sts at
beg of next 2 rows. 62 (62: 64: 64: 66) sts.
Dec 1 st at each end of next 3 rows, then on
every foll alt row until 44 sts rem, then on foll 7
rows, ending with a WS row. 30 sts.
Cast off 3 sts at beg of next 4 rows.
Cast off rem 18 sts.

MAKING UP
PRESS as described on the information page.
Join right shoulder seam using back stitch, or
mattress st if preferred.
Neckband
With RS facing, using 3¼mm (US 3) needles
and yarn A, pick up and knit 12 sts down left side
of front neck, 20 (22: 22: 24: 24) sts from front,
12 sts up right side of front neck, 12 sts down
right side of back neck, 20 (22: 22: 24: 24) sts
from back, then 12 sts up left side of back neck.
88 (92: 92: 96: 96) sts.
Cast off knitwise (on **WS**).
See information page for finishing instructions,
setting in sleeves using the set-in method.

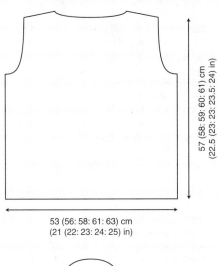

57 (58: 59: 60: 61) cm
(22.5 (23: 23: 23.5: 24) in)

53 (56: 58: 61: 63) cm
(21 (22: 23: 24: 25) in)

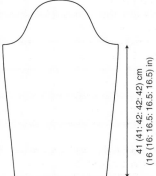

41 (41: 42: 42: 42) cm
(16 (16: 16.5: 16.5: 16.5) in)

MILLER

KIM HARGREAVES

YARN

	ladies			mens			
	S	M	L	M	L	XL	
To fit bust/chest	86	91	97	102	107	112	cm
	34	36	38	40	42	44	in

Rowan Yorkshire Tweed DK

A	8	9	10	12	13	14 x 50gm
B	1	1	1	1	1	1 x 50gm

(ladies photographed in A – Frolic 350 and
B – Cheer 343, mans in A – Champion 346 and
B – Skip 347)

NEEDLES

1 pair 3¼mm (no 10) (US 3) needles
1 pair 4mm (no 8) (US 6) needles

TENSION

20 sts and 28 rows to 10 cm measured over
stocking stitch using 4mm (US 6) needles.

Pattern note: The pattern is written for the
3 ladies sizes, followed by the mens sizes in **bold**.
Where only one figure appears this applies to all
sizes in that group.

BACK

Cast on 87 (95: 101: **109: 115: 123**) sts using
3¼mm (US 3) needles and yarn A.
Row 1 (RS): K1, ★P1, K1, rep from ★ to end.
Row 2: P1, ★K1, P1, rep from ★ to end.
These 2 rows form rib.
Work in rib for a further 14 rows, ending with a
WS row.
Change to 4mm (US 6) needles.
Next row (RS): K2, M1, K to last 2 sts, M1, K2.
Beg with a **purl** row and working all increases as
set by last row, cont in st st, shaping side seams by
inc 1 st at each end of every foll 12th (**16th**) row
until there are 97 (105: 111: **119: 125: 133**) sts.
Cont straight until back measures 28 (**39**) cm,
ending with a WS row.
Shape armholes
Cast off 5 (**6**) sts at beg of next 2 rows.
87 (95: 101: **107: 113: 121**) sts.
Dec 1 st at each end of next 5 rows, then on foll
3 (4: 4: **4: 4: 5**) alt rows. 71 (77: 83: **89: 95: 101**) sts.
Cont straight until armhole measures 20 (21: 22:
23: 24: 25) cm, ending with a WS row.
Shape shoulders and back neck
Cast off 7 (7: 8: **9: 9: 10**) sts at beg of next 2 rows.
57 (63: 67: **71: 77: 81**) sts.
Next row (RS): Cast off 7 (7: 8: **9: 9: 10**) sts,
K until there are 10 (12: 12: **12: 14: 14**) sts on
right needle and turn, leaving rem sts on a holder.
Work each side of neck separately.
Cast off 4 sts at beg of next row.
Cast off rem 6 (8: 8: **8: 10: 10**) sts.
With RS facing, rejoin yarn to rem sts, cast off
centre 23 (25: 27: **29: 31: 33**) sts, K to end.
Complete to match first side, reversing shapings.

FRONT

Work as given for back until armhole measures
7 (**8**) cm, ending with a WS row.
Divide for front opening
Next row (RS): K33 (36: 39: **42: 45: 48**) and
turn, leaving rem sts on a holder.
Work each side of neck separately.
Cont straight until 15 (**17**) rows less have been
worked than on back to start of shoulder
shaping, ending with a RS row.
Shape neck
Cast off 4 (5: 6: **7: 8: 9**) sts at beg of next row.
29 (31: 33: **35: 37: 39**) sts.
Dec 1 st at neck edge of next 6 rows, then on
foll 3 alt rows. 20 (22: 24: **26: 28: 30**) sts.
Work 2 (**4**) rows, ending with a WS row.
Shape shoulder
Cast off 7 (7: 8: **9: 9: 10**) sts at beg of next and
foll alt row.
Work 1 row. Cast off rem 6 (8: 8: **8: 10: 10**) sts.
With RS facing, slip centre 5 sts onto a holder,
rejoin yarn to rem sts, K to end.
Complete to match first side, reversing shapings.

SLEEVES (both alike)

Cast on 51 (55: 59: **63: 67: 71**) sts using 3¼mm
(US 3) needles and yarn B.
Work in rib as given for back for 1 row.
Break off yarn B and join in yarn A.
Cont in rib for a further 17 rows, ending with a
WS row.
Change to 4mm (US 6) needles.
Beg with a K row and working all increases 2 sts
in from ends of rows as given for back, cont in
st st, shaping sides by inc 1 st at each end of 3rd
and every foll 12th (12th: 14th: **12th**) row to
59 (69: 63: **71: 81: 91**) sts, then on every foll
10th (10th: 12th: **10th**) row to 69 (73: 77: **85:
89: 93**) sts.

Cont straight until sleeve measures 43 (45: 47:
50: 52: 54) cm, ending with a **RS** row.
Shape top
Cast off 5 (**6**) sts at beg of next 2 rows.
59 (63: 67: **73: 77: 81**) sts.
Dec 1 st at each end of next 3 rows, then on
foll 2 alt rows, then on every foll 4th row until
37 (41: 45: **51: 55: 59**) sts rem.
Work 1 row.
Dec 1 st at each end of next and foll 0 (**2**) alt
rows, then on every row until 25 (**35**) sts rem,
ending with a WS row.
Cast off rem 25 (**35**) sts.

MAKING UP

PRESS as described on the information page.
Join both shoulder seams using back stitch, or
mattress st if preferred.
Left front band
Ladies version only
Cast on 5 sts using 3¼mm (US 3) needles and
yarn A.
Mans version only
Slip 5 sts from holder at base of front opening
onto 3¼mm (US 3) needles and rejoin yarn A
with RS facing.
Both versions
Row 1 (RS): K2, P1, K2.
Row 2: K1, (P1, K1) twice.
Rep these 2 rows until band, when slightly
stretched, fits up left side of front opening to
neck shaping, ending with a WS row.
Break yarn and leave sts on a holder.
Right front band
Ladies version only
Slip 5 sts from holder at base of front opening
onto 3¼mm (US 3) needles and rejoin yarn A
with RS facing.
Mans version only
Cast on 5 sts using 3¼mm (US 3) needles and
yarn A.

48.5 (52.5: 55.5: **59.5: 62.5: 66.5**) cm
(19 (20.5: 22: **23.5: 24.5: 26**) in)

48 (49: 50: **62: 63: 64**) cm
(19 (19.5: 19.5: **24.5: 25: 25**) in)

43 (45: 47: **50: 52: 54**) cm
(17 (17.5: 18.5: **19.5: 20.5: 21.5**) in)

Both versions

Cont as given for left front band until this band, when slightly stretched, fits up right side of front opening to neck shaping, ending with a WS row. Do NOT break yarn.

Collar

With RS facing, using 3¼mm (US 3) needles and yarn A, rib across 5 sts from right front band, pick up and knit 26 (27: 28: **28: 29: 30**) sts up right side of neck, 35 (37: 39: **41: 43: 45**) sts from back, and 26 (27: 28: **28: 29: 30**) sts down left side of neck, then rib across 5 sts of left front band. 97 (101: 105: **107: 111: 115**) sts. Keeping rib correct as set by bands, work in rib for a further 22 rows.

Join in yarn B.

Using yarn B, work 2 rows.

Using yarn A, work 2 rows.

Rep last 2 rows twice more.

Break off yarn B.

Using yarn A, work a further 2 rows.

Cast off in rib.

See information page for finishing instructions, setting in sleeves using the set-in method. Slip stitch cast-on edge of one front band in place behind other front band at base of front opening.

Design number 19

CHARLOTTE

KIM HARGREAVES

YARN

	XS	S	M	L	XL
To fit bust	81	86	91	97	102 cm
	32	34	36	38	40 in

Rowan Yorkshire Tweed Aran

| | | 5 | 6 | 6 | 6 | 7 x 100gm |

(photographed in Muffin 413)

NEEDLES

1 pair 3¾mm (no 9) (US 5) needles
1 pair 4mm (no 8) (US 6) needles
1 pair 5mm (no 6) (US 8) needles

BUCKLE - 3.5 cm (1¼ in) buckle

TENSION

16 sts and 23 rows to 10 cm measured over stocking stitch using 5mm (US 8) needles.

SPECIAL ABBREVIATIONS

Right dec = Sl 1, K1, psso, slip this st back onto left needle and lift 2nd st on left needle over this st and off needle, slip same st back onto right needle - 2 sts decreased

Left dec = Sl 1, K2tog, psso - 2 sts decreased

BACK

Cast on 73 (77: 81: 85: 89) sts using 4mm (US 6) needles.

Row 1 (RS): K1, *P1, K1, rep from * to end.

Row 2: As row 1.

These 2 rows form moss st.

Cont in moss st for a further 24 rows, ending with a WS row.

Change to 5mm (US 8) needles.

Beg with a K row, work in st st for 2 rows, ending with a WS row.

Place markers on 19th (20th: 21st: 22nd: 23rd) st in from both ends of last row.

Next row (dec) (RS): K2, K2tog, K to within 1 st of first marked st, right dec (marked st is centre st of this group of 3 sts), K to within 1 st of next marked st, left dec (marked st is centre st of this group of 3 sts), K to last 4 sts, K2tog tbl, K2. 67 (71: 75: 79: 83) sts.

Work 7 rows.

Rep the dec row once more.

61 (65: 69: 73: 77) sts.

Work 13 rows, ending with a WS row.

Next row (inc) (RS): K2, M1, (K to marked st, M1, K marked st, M1) twice, K to last 2 sts, M1, K2. 67 (71: 75: 79: 83) sts.

Rep last 14 rows once more.

73 (77: 81: 85: 89) sts.

Cont straight until back measures 35 (36: 36: 37: 37) cm, ending with a **RS** row.

Place marker on centre st of last row.

Next row (WS): P to marked centre st, K marked st, P to end.

Next row: K to within 1 st of marked st, P1, K marked st, P1, K to end.

Next row: P to within 2 sts of marked st, (K1, P1) twice, K1, P to end.

Next row: K to within 3 sts of marked st, (P1, K1) 3 times, P1, K to end.

Next row: P to within 4 sts of marked st, (K1, P1) 4 times, K1, P to end.

Last 4 rows set the sts - centre sts in moss st with side sts in st st.

Shape armholes

Working 2 extra sts in moss st on every row as now set, cast off 3 (4: 4: 5: 5) sts at beg of next 2 rows. 67 (69: 73: 75: 79) sts.

Dec 1 st at each end of next 3 (3: 5: 5: 7) rows, then on foll 3 alt rows. 55 (57: 57: 59: 59) sts.

Cont to work 2 extra sts in moss st on every row until all sts are in moss st, and then cont straight in moss st until armhole measures 20 (20: 21: 21: 22) cm, ending with a WS row.

Shape shoulders and back neck

Cast off 5 sts at beg of next 2 rows.

45 (47: 47: 49: 49) sts.

Next row (RS): Cast off 5 sts, moss st until there are 10 sts on right needle and turn, leaving rem sts on a holder.

Work each side of neck separately.

Cast off 4 sts at beg of next row.

Cast off rem 6 sts.

With RS facing, slip centre 15 (17: 17: 19: 19) sts onto a holder, rejoin yarn to rem sts, moss st to end.

Complete to match first side, reversing shapings.

FRONT

Work as given for back until 12 (12: 12: 14: 14) rows less have been worked than on back to start of shoulder shaping, ending with a WS row.

Shape neck

Next row (RS): Moss st 23 (23: 23: 24: 24) sts and turn, leaving rem sts on a holder.

Work each side of neck separately.

Dec 1 st at neck edge of next 4 rows, then on foll 3 (3: 3: 4: 4) alt rows. 16 sts.

Work 1 row, ending with a WS row.

Shape shoulder

Cast off 5 sts at beg of next and foll alt row.

Work 1 row. Cast off rem 6 sts.

With RS facing, slip centre 9 (11: 11: 11: 11) sts onto a holder, rejoin yarn to rem sts, moss st to end.

Complete to match first side, reversing shapings.

SLEEVES (both alike)

Cast on 37 (37: 39: 41: 41) sts using 4mm (US 6) needles.

Work in moss st as given for back for 22 rows, inc 1 st at each end of 17th of these rows and ending with a WS row. 39 (39: 41: 43: 43) sts.

Change to 5mm (US 8) needles.

Beg with a K row, work in st st for 6 (4: 4: 4: 4) rows, ending with a WS row.

Next row (RS): K2, M1, K to last 2 sts, M1, K2.

Working all increases as set by last row, inc 1 st at each end of every foll 12th (10th: 10th: 10th: 10th) row to 43 (49: 53: 55: 47) sts, then on every foll 10th (8th: 8th: 8th: 8th) row until there are 53 (55: 57: 59: 61) sts.

Cont straight until sleeve measures 43 (43: 44: 44: 44) cm, ending with a WS row.

Shape top

Cast off 3 (4: 4: 5: 5) sts at beg of next 2 rows.

47 (47: 49: 49: 51) sts.

Dec 1 st at each end of next 2 rows.

43 (43: 45: 45: 47) sts.

Place marker on centre st of last row.

Next row (RS): K2tog, K to marked st, P marked st, K to last 2 sts, K2tog.

Next row: P to within 1 st of marked st, K1, P marked st, K1, P to end.

Next row: K2tog, K to within 2 sts of marked st, (P1, K1) twice, P1, K to last 2 sts, K2tog.

39 (39: 41: 41: 43) sts.

Next row: P to within 3 sts of marked st, (K1, P1) 3 times, K1, P to end.

Last 4 rows set the sts - centre sts in moss st with side sts in st st.

Working 2 extra sts in moss st on every row as now set until all sts are worked in moss st and then completing sleeve in moss st, cont as folls:

Dec 1 st at each end of 3rd and every foll 4th row until 31 (31: 33: 33: 35) sts rem.

Work 1 row, ending with a WS row.

Dec 1 st at each end of next and every foll alt row until 27 sts rem, then on foll 5 rows, ending with a WS row. Cast off rem 17 sts.

MAKING UP

PRESS as described on the information page.

Join right shoulder seam using back stitch, or mattress st if preferred.

Collar

With RS facing and using 4mm (US 6) needles, pick up and knit 15 (15: 15: 16: 16) sts down left side of front neck, moss st 9 (11: 11: 11: 11) sts from front holder, pick up and knit 16 (16: 16: 17: 17) sts up right side of front neck, and 4 sts down right side of back neck, moss st 15 (17: 17: 19: 19) sts from back holder, then pick up and knit 4 sts up left side of back neck.
63 (67: 67: 71: 71) sts.

Row 1 (WS): K1 (0: 0: 1: 1), *P1, K1, rep from * to last 0 (1: 1: 0: 0) st, P0 (1: 1: 0: 0).
This row sets position of moss st.
Work in moss st for a further 2 rows, ending with a WS row.

Next row (RS): Moss st 18 (19: 19: 20: 20) sts, work 2 tog and turn, leaving rem sts on a holder.
Work each side of neck separately.
Cont in moss st on these 19 (20: 20: 21: 21) sts until collar measures 12 cm from pick-up row.
Cast off in moss st.
With RS facing, rejoin yarn to rem 43 (46: 46: 49: 49) sts, moss st to end.
Cont in moss st on these 43 (46: 46: 49: 49) sts until collar measures 12 cm from pick-up row.
Cast off in moss st.

Belt

Cast on 7 sts using 3¾mm (US 5) needles.

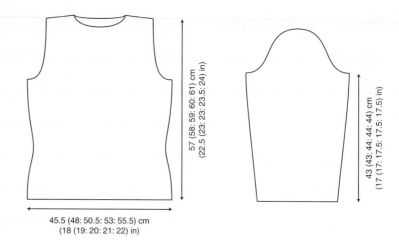

45.5 (48: 50.5: 53: 55.5) cm
(18 (19: 20: 21: 22) in)

Work in moss st as given for back until belt measures 115 cm. Cast off.

Belt tab

Cast on 23 sts using 3¾mm (US 5) needles.
Work in moss st as given for back for one row.
Cast off in moss st.

See information page for finishing instructions, setting in sleeves using the set-in method and reversing collar seam for turn-back. Attach buckle to one end of belt. Join ends of belt tab and thread tab over belt, securing it at the back approx 14 cm from buckle.

Design number 20

CABLE ROSE

SASHA KAGAN

YARN

	XS	S	M	L	XL	
To fit bust	81	86	91	97	102cm	
	32	34	36	38	40 in	

Rowan Yorkshire Tweed 4 ply

A Desiccated	263	13	13	14	15	15 x 25gm
B Barley	264	2	2	2	2	2 x 25gm
C Brilliant	274	3	3	3	3	3 x 25gm
D Foxy	275	3	3	3	3	3 x 25gm
E Blessed	269	3	3	3	4	4 x 25gm

NEEDLES

1 pair 2¾mm (no 12) (US 2) needles
1 pair 3¼mm (no 10) (US 3) needles
2¾mm (no 12) (US 2) circular needle
Cable needle

BUTTONS – 8 x 75320

TENSION

26 sts and 38 rows to 10 cm measured over stocking stitch using 3¼mm (US 3) needles.

SPECIAL ABBREVIATIONS

C4B = Cable 4 back Slip next 2 sts onto cable needle and leave at back of work, K2, then K2 from cable needle
C4F = Cable 4 front Slip next 2 sts onto cable needle and leave at front of work, K2, then K2 from cable needle

BACK

Cast on 101 (107: 113: 119: 125) sts using 2¾mm (US 2) needles and yarn A.
Row 1 (RS): K1 tbl, *P1, K1 tbl, rep from * to end.
Row 2: P1, *K1 tbl, P1, rep from * to end.
These 2 rows form rib.
Cont in rib for a further 5 rows, ending with a RS row.
Row 8 (WS): Rib 6 (4: 2: 12: 11), *M1, rib 2, M1, rib 3 (3: 3: 2: 2), rep from * to last 5 (3: 1: 11: 10) sts, M1, rib to end.
138 (148: 158: 168: 178) sts.
Change to 3¼mm (US 3) needles.
Using the **intarsia** technique as described on the information page, starting and ending rows as indicated and repeating the 28 row repeat throughout, cont in patt from chart as folls:
Work 6 rows, ending with a WS row.

Inc 1 st at each end of next and every foll 10th row until there are 158 (168: 178: 188: 198) sts, taking inc sts into patt.
Cont straight until back measures 30 (31: 31: 32: 32) cm, ending with a WS row.

Shape armholes

Keeping patt correct, cast off 9 (10: 10: 11: 11) sts at beg of next 2 rows.
140 (148: 158: 166: 176) sts.
Dec 1 st at each end of next 5 (5: 7: 7: 9) rows, then on foll 1 (3: 4: 6: 7) alt rows, then on every foll 4th row until 124 (128: 132: 136: 140) sts rem.
Cont straight until armhole measures 20 (20: 21: 21: 22) cm, ending with a WS row.

Shape shoulders and back neck

Cast off 12 (12: 13: 13: 14) sts at beg of next 2 rows.
100 (104: 106: 110: 112) sts.
Next row (RS): Cast off 12 (12: 13: 13: 14) sts, patt until there are 15 (16: 16: 17: 17) sts on right needle and turn, leaving rem sts on a holder.
Work each side of neck separately.
Cast off 4 sts at beg of next row.
Cast off rem 11 (12: 12: 13: 13) sts.
With RS facing, rejoin yarns to rem sts, cast off centre 46 (48: 48: 50: 50) sts, patt to end.
Complete to match first side, reversing shapings.

LEFT FRONT

Cast on 51 (55: 57: 61: 63) sts using 2¾mm (US 2) needles and yarn A.
Work in rib as given for back for 7 rows, ending with a RS row.
Row 8 (WS): Rib 3 (4: 1: 8: 6), *M1, rib 2, M1, rib 3 (3: 3: 2: 2), rep from * to last 3 (1: 1: 5: 5) sts, (M1) 1 (0: 1: 0: 1) times, rib to end.
70 (75: 80: 85: 90) sts.

76

Change to 3¼mm (US 3) needles.

Starting and ending rows as indicated, cont in patt from chart as folls:

Work 6 rows, ending with a WS row.

Inc 1 st at beg of next and every foll 10th row until there are 80 (85: 90: 95: 100) sts, taking inc sts into patt.

Cont straight until left front matches back to beg of armhole shaping, ending with a WS row.

Shape armhole and front slope

Keeping patt correct, cast off 9 (10: 10: 11: 11) sts at beg and dec 1 st at end of next row.

70 (74: 79: 83: 88) sts.

Work 1 row.

Dec 1 st at armhole edge of next 5 (5: 7: 7: 9) rows, then on foll 1 (3: 4: 6: 7) alt rows, then on 2 foll 4th rows **and at same time** dec 1 st at front slope edge of next and every foll alt row.

54 sts.

Dec 1 st at front slope edge **only** on 2nd and foll 12 (12: 8: 8: 4) alt rows, then on every foll 4th row until 35 (36: 38: 39: 41) sts rem.

Cont straight until left front matches back to start of shoulder shaping, ending with a WS row.

Shape shoulder

Cast off 12 (12: 13: 13: 14) sts at beg of next and foll alt row.

Work 1 row.

Cast off rem 11 (12: 12: 13: 13) sts.

RIGHT FRONT

Cast on 51 (55: 57: 61: 63) sts using 2¾mm (US 2) needles and yarn A.

Work in rib as given for back for 7 rows, ending with a RS row.

Row 8 (WS): Rib 3 (4: 1: 8: 6), ★M1, rib 2, M1, rib 3 (3: 3: 2: 2), rep from ★ to last 3 (1: 1: 5: 5) sts, (M1) 1 (0: 1: 0: 1) times, rib to end.

70 (75: 80: 85: 90) sts.

Change to 3¼mm (US 3) needles.

Starting and ending rows as indicated, cont in patt from chart as folls:

Work 6 rows, ending with a WS row.

Inc 1 st at end of next and every foll 10th row until there are 80 (85: 90: 95: 100) sts, taking inc sts into patt.

Complete to match left front, reversing shapings.

SLEEVES (both alike)

Cast on 57 (57: 59: 61: 61) sts using 2¾mm (US 2) needles and yarn A.

Work in rib as given for back for 7 rows, ending with a RS row.

Row 8 (WS): Rib 7 (7: 8: 9: 9), ★M1, rib 1, M1, rib 2, M1, rib 1, rib 6, rep from ★ to last 10 (10: 11: 12: 12) sts, M1, rib 1, M1, rib 2, M1, rib 1, M1, rib to last st, inc in last st.

78 (78: 80: 82: 82) sts.

Change to 3¼mm (US 3) needles.

Starting and ending rows as indicated, cont in patt from chart, shaping sides by inc 1 st at each end of 7th and every foll 6th (6th: 6th: 6th: 4th) row to 118 (126: 132: 134: 94) sts, then on every foll 8th (8th: –: –: 6th) row until there are 126 (128: –: –: 138) sts, taking inc sts into patt.

Cont straight until sleeve measures 45 (45: 46: 46: 46) cm, ending with a WS row.

Shape top

Keeping patt correct, cast off 9 (10: 10: 11: 11) sts at beg of next 2 rows.

108 (108: 112: 112: 116) sts.

Dec 1 st at each end of next 5 rows, then on foll 5 alt rows, then on every foll 4th row until 84 (84: 88: 88: 92) sts rem.

Work 1 row, ending with a WS row.

Dec 1 st at each end of next and every foll alt row to 74 sts, then on foll 3 rows, ending with a WS row. 68 sts.

Cast off 3 sts at beg of next 6 rows, then 8 sts at beg of foll 4 rows.

Cast off rem 18 sts.

MAKING UP

PRESS as described on the information page. Join both shoulder seams using back stitch, or mattress st if preferred.

Front band

With RS facing, using 2¾mm (US 2) circular needle and yarn A, starting and ending at cast-on edges, pick up and knit 85 (87: 87: 89: 89) sts up right front opening edge to start of front slope shaping, 75 (75: 78: 78: 81) sts up right front slope to shoulder, 45 (47: 47: 49: 49) sts from back,

75 (75: 78: 78: 81) sts down left front slope to start of front slope shaping, then 85 (87: 87: 89: 89) sts down left front opening edge.

365 (371: 377: 383: 389) sts.

Work in rib as given for back for 3 rows.

Row 4 (RS): Rib 2 (3: 3: 4: 4), ★work 2 tog, yrn (to make a buttonhole), rib 10, rep from ★ 6 times more, work 2 tog, yrn (to make 8th buttonhole), rib to end.

Work in rib for a further 2 rows.

Cast off in rib (on **WS**).

See information page for finishing instructions, setting in sleeves using the set-in method.

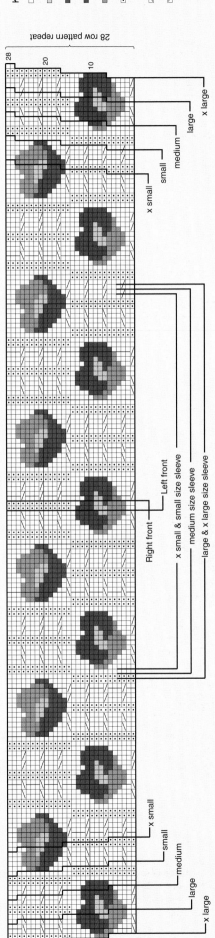

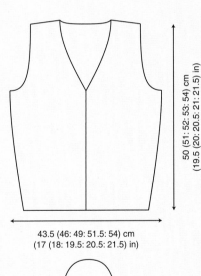

50 (51: 52: 53: 54) cm
(19.5 (20: 20.5: 21: 21.5) in)

43.5 (46: 49: 51.5: 54) cm
(17 (18: 19.5: 20.5: 21.5) in)

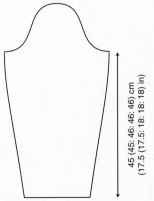

45 (45: 46: 46: 46) cm
(17.5 (17.5: 18: 18: 18) in)

RENAISSANCE

KIM HARGREAVES

YARN

	XS	S	M	L	XL	
To fit bust	81	86	91	97	102	cm
	32	34	36	38	40	in

Rowan Yorkshire Tweed Aran and Yorkshire Tweed 4 ply

A Aran Muffin 413	5	6	6	6	7	x 100gm
B Aran Thorny 412	5	5	5	6	6	x 100gm
C 4 ply Knight 281	4	4	4	5	5	x 25gm

NEEDLES

1 pair 4mm (no 8) (US 6) needles
1 pair 5mm (no 6) (US 8) needles
3¼mm (no 10) (US 3) long circular needle

TENSION

Yorkshire Tweed Aran: 16 sts and 23 rows to 10 cm measured over stocking stitch using 5mm (US 8) needles.
Yorkshire Tweed 4 ply: 26 sts and 38 rows to 10 cm measured over stocking stitch using 3¼mm (US 3) needles.

BACK and FRONT (worked in one piece to armholes)

Cast on 148 (156: 164: 172: 180) sts using 4mm (US 6) needles and yarn B.
Beg with a K row, work in st st for 9 rows, ending with a **RS** row.
Row 10 (WS): Knit (to form fold line).
Change to 5mm (US 8) needles.
Join in yarn A.
Using the **intarsia** technique as described on the information page, and starting and ending rows as indicated, cont in patt from chart for back and fronts, which is worked entirely in st st beg with a K row, as folls:
Cont straight until chart row 110 has been completed, ending with a WS row.
Divide for armholes
Next row (RS): Patt 27 (28: 30: 31: 33) sts and slip these sts onto a holder for right front, cast off next 8 (10: 10: 12: 12) sts, patt until there are 78 (80: 84: 86: 90) sts on right needle and slip these sts onto another holder for back, cast off next 8 (10: 10: 12: 12) sts, patt to end.

Chart for back and front

Work on this last set of 27 (28: 30: 31: 33) sts only for left front as folls:
Work 1 row.
Dec 1 st at armhole edge of next 2 rows. 25 (26: 28: 29: 31) sts.

Shape front slope
Dec 1 st at armhole edge of next 1 (1: 3: 3: 5) rows, then on foll 4 alt rows **and at same time** dec 1 st at front slope edge of next and foll 0 (0: 0: 10th: 10th) row. 19 (20: 20: 20: 20) sts.
Cont foll chart until all 158 rows of chart have been completed and then complete work in st st using yarn A only **and at same time** dec 1 st at front slope edge **only** on 12th (4th: 4th: 10th: 10th) and every foll 20th (14th: 14th: 12th: 12th) row until 17 (17: 18: 17: 17) sts rem, then on foll – (–: 16th: –: –) row. 17 sts.
Cont straight until armhole measures 23 (23: 24: 24: 25) cm, ending with a WS row.

Shape shoulder
Cast off 6 sts at beg of next and foll alt row.
Work 1 row.
Cast off rem 5 sts.

Shape back
Rejoin yarns to 78 (80: 84: 86: 90) sts left on back holder with WS facing and work 1 row.
Keeping patt correct, dec 1 st at each end of next 3 (3: 5: 5: 7) rows, then on foll 4 alt rows. 64 (66: 66: 68: 68) sts.
Cont straight until all 158 rows of chart have been completed and then cont in st st using yarn A only until 2 rows less have been worked than on left front to start of shoulder shaping, ending with a WS row.

Shape back neck and shoulders
Next row (RS): Patt 20 sts and turn, leaving rem sts on a holder.
Work each side of neck separately.
Dec 1 st at neck edge of next row. 19 sts.
Cast off 6 sts at beg and dec 1 st at end of next row.
Work 1 row.
Rep last 2 rows once more.

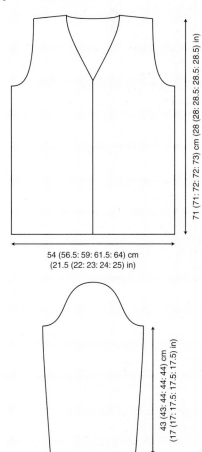

71 (71: 72: 72: 73) cm (28 (28: 28.5: 28.5: 28.5) in)

54 (56.5: 59: 61.5: 64) cm
(21.5 (22: 23: 24: 25) in)

43 (43: 44: 44: 44) cm
(17 (17: 17.5: 17.5: 17.5) in)

Cast off rem 5 sts.
With RS facing, rejoin yarns to rem sts, cast off centre 24 (26: 26: 28: 28) sts, patt to end.
Complete to match first side, reversing shapings.

Shape right front
Rejoin yarns to 27 (28: 30: 31: 33) sts left on right front holder with WS facing and work 1 row. Keeping patt correct, complete to match left front, reversing shapings.

LEFT SLEEVE
Cast on 53 (53: 55: 57: 57) sts using 5mm (US 8) needles and yarn A.
Starting and ending rows as indicated, cont in patt from chart for left sleeve, inc 1 st at each end of 41st (25th: 25th: 25th: 21st) and every foll 0 (24th: 24th: 24th: 20th) row until there are 55 (57: 59: 61: 63) sts.
Cont straight until chart row 76 (76: 78: 78: 78) has been completed, ending with a WS row. (Sleeve should measure 33 (33: 34: 34: 34) cm.)

Shape top
Keeping patt correct, cast off 4 (5: 5: 6: 6) sts at beg of next 2 rows. 47 (47: 49: 49: 51) sts.
Dec 1 st at each end of next 3 rows, then on every foll 4th row until 31 (31: 33: 33: 35) sts rem.
Work 1 row, ending with a WS row.
Dec 1 st at each end of next and every foll alt row until 23 sts rem, then on foll row, ending with a WS row. Cast off rem 21 sts.

RIGHT SLEEVE
Work to match left sleeve, foll chart for right sleeve.

MAKING UP
PRESS as described on the information page.
Join both shoulder seams using back stitch, or mattress st if preferred.

Front band
Cast on 22 sts using 4mm (US 6) needles and yarn B.
Cont in herringbone patt as folls:
Row 1 (WS): Purl.
Row 2: *K2tog, K2, inc in next st as folls: place point of right needle down through the (purled) head of st below next st and K into this loop then K the st above, K2, rep from * to last st, K1.
Row 3: Purl.
Row 4: K1, *K2, inc in next st (as detailed on row 1), K2, K2tog, rep from * to end.
These 4 rows form herringbone patt.
Cont in patt until front band, when very slightly stretched, fits up right front opening edge from fold line row to start of front slope shaping, up right front slope, across back neck, down left front slope, and then down left front opening edge to fold line row, ending with a WS row.
Cast off.
Slip stitch band in place.

Cuffs (both alike)
Work as given for front band, making a strip to fit across cast-on edge of each sleeve.
Slip stitch cuffs in place.

Front band facing
With RS facing, using 3¼mm (US 3) circular needle and yarn C, pick up and knit 436 (439: 444: 447: 452) sts evenly along entire free row end edge of front band.
(**Note**: you may need to adjust this number of sts to ensure facing lays flat. If necessary, place pins along edge every 10 cm and pick up 26 sts between each pair of pins, picking up a proportionate amount at end of band.)
Row 1 (WS): Knit (to form fold line).
Beg with a K row, work in st st for 10 cm. Cast off.

Fold front band facing to inside and slip stitch in place.

Cuff facings (both alike)
With RS facing, using 3¼mm (US 3) circular needle and yarn C, pick up and knit 86 (86: 89: 92: 92) sts evenly along free row end edge of cuff.
Row 1 (WS): Knit (to form fold line).

Beg with a K row, work in st st for 10 cm. Cast off.
Belt
Cast on 3 sts using 4mm (US 6) needles and yarn B.
Row 1 (RS): K1, P1, K1.
Row 2: As row 1.
These 2 rows form moss st.

Left sleeve

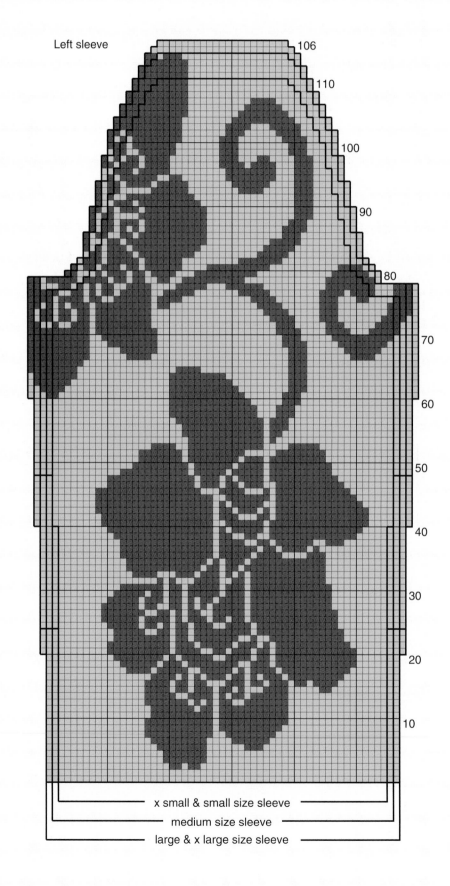

106
110
100
90
80
70
60
50
40
30
20
10

x small & small size sleeve
medium size sleeve
large & x large size sleeve

Cont in moss st, inc 1 st at each end of next and every foll alt row until there are 9 sts.
Cont straight until belt measures 130 cm, ending with a WS row.
Dec 1 st at each end of next and every foll alt row until 3 sts rem.
Work 1 row. Cast off in moss st.

See information page for finishing instructions, setting in sleeves using the set-in method. Fold first 9 rows of body to inside along fold line row and slip stitch in place. Fold cuff facings to inside along fold line rows and slip stitch in place.
Using yarn B, make two 20 cm long tassels attach to ends of belt.

JANE

KIM HARGREAVES

YARN

	XS	S	M	L	XL	
To fit bust	81	86	91	97	102	cm
	32	34	36	38	40	in

Rowan Yorkshire Tweed Aran and 4 ply

A Aran Tusk	4	17	4	4	4	5	5 x 100gm
B 4 ply Sheer	2	67	3	3	3	4	4 x 25gm
C 4 ply Barley	2	64	2	2	2	2	2 x 25gm

Oddments of Yorkshire Tweed 4 ply in each of yarn D (Highlander 266) and yarn E (Radiant 276) for flower

NEEDLES

1 pair 2¼mm (no 13) (US 1) needles
1 pair 2¾mm (no 12) (US 2) needles
1 pair 3mm (no 11) (US 2/3) needles
1 pair 5mm (no 6) (US 8) needles

BUTTONS

7 x 75320

TENSION

16 sts and 23 rows to 10 cm measured over stocking stitch using 5mm (US 8) needles and yarn A.

BACK

Cast on 121 (127: 133: 139: 145) sts using 2¾mm (US 2) needles and yarn B.
**Beg with a K row, work in st st for 12 rows, ending with a WS row.
Place markers at both ends of last row.
Change to 3mm (US 2/3) needles.
Row 13 (RS): Using yarn B, knit.
Join in yarn C.
Row 14: Using yarn C, purl.
Rows 15 to 24: As rows 13 and 14, 5 times.
Break off yarns B and C and join in yarn A.
Change to 5mm (US 8) needles.**
Next row (RS): K0 (1: 2: 2: 3), *K2tog, K1, K2tog, rep from * to last 1 (1: 1: 2: 2) sts, K1 (1: 1: 2: 2). 73 (77: 81: 85: 89) sts.
Beg with a **purl** row, cont in st st as folls:
Work 5 rows, ending with a WS row.
Next row (RS): K2, K2tog, K to last 4 sts, K2tog tbl, K2.

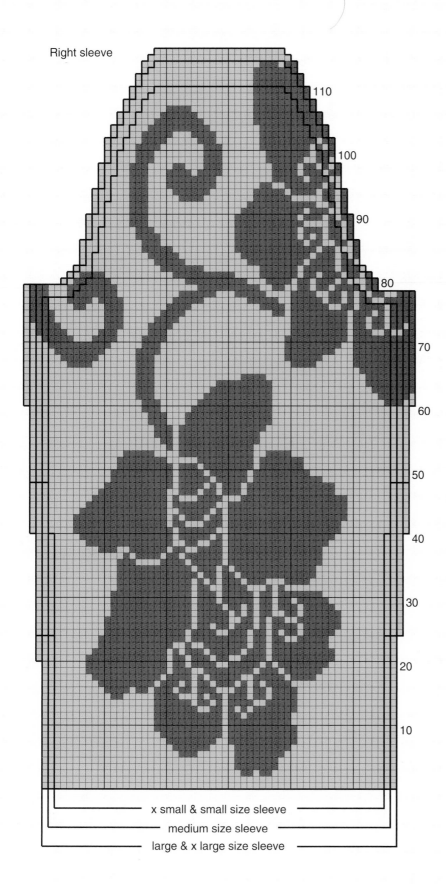

Right sleeve

110

100

90

80

70

60

50

40

30

20

10

x small & small size sleeve
medium size sleeve
large & x large size sleeve

Working all decreases as set by last row, dec 1 st at each end of every foll 4th row until 63 (67: 71: 75: 79) sts rem.

Work 11 rows, ending with a WS row.

Next row (RS): K2, M1, K to last 2 sts, M1, K2.

Working all increases as set by last row, inc 1 st at each end of every foll 6th row until there are 73 (77: 81: 85: 89) sts.

Cont straight until back measures 35 (36: 36: 37: 37) cm **from markers**, ending with a WS row.

Shape armholes

Cast off 3 (4: 4: 5: 5) sts at beg of next 2 rows. 67 (69: 73: 75: 79) sts.

Dec 1 st at each end of next 3 (3: 5: 5: 7) rows, then on foll 3 alt rows. 55 (57: 57: 59: 59) sts.

Cont straight until armhole measures 20 (20: 21: 21: 22) cm, ending with a WS row.

Shape shoulders and back neck

Cast off 5 sts at beg of next 2 rows. 45 (47: 47: 49: 49) sts.

Next row (RS): Cast off 5 sts, K until there are 9 (10: 10: 10: 10) sts on right needle and turn, leaving rem sts on a holder.

Work each side of neck separately.

Cast off 4 sts at beg of next row.

Cast off rem 5 (6: 6: 6: 6) sts.

With RS facing, rejoin yarn to rem sts, cast off centre 17 (17: 17: 19: 19) sts, K to end.

Complete to match first side, reversing shapings.

LEFT FRONT

Cast on 61 (65: 67: 71: 73) sts using 2¾mm (US 2) needles and yarn B.

Work as given for back from ★★ to ★★.

Next row (RS): K0 (0: 1: 0: 2), *K2tog, K1, K2tog, rep from * to last 1 (0: 1: 1: 1) sts, K1 (0: 1: 1: 1). 37 (39: 41: 43: 45) sts.

Beg with a **purl** row and working all side seam shaping 2 sts in from ends of rows as given for back, cont in st st, dec 1 st at beg of 6th and every foll 4th row until 32 (34: 36: 38: 40) sts rem.

Work 11 rows, ending with a WS row.

Inc 1 st at beg of next and every foll 6th row until there are 37 (39: 41: 43: 45) sts.

Cont straight until left front matches back to beg of armhole shaping, ending with a WS row.

Shape armhole

Cast off 3 (4: 4: 5: 5) sts at beg of next row. 34 (35: 37: 38: 40) sts.

Work 1 row.

Dec 1 st at armhole edge of next 3 (3: 5: 5: 7) rows, then on foll 3 alt rows. 28 (29: 29: 30: 30) sts.

Cont straight until 13 (13: 13: 15: 15) rows less have been worked than on back to start of shoulder shaping, ending with a RS row.

Shape neck

Cast off 6 sts at beg of next row. 22 (23: 23: 24: 24) sts.

Dec 1 st at neck edge of next 5 rows, then on foll 2 (2: 2: 3: 3) alt rows. 15 (16: 16: 16: 16) sts.

Work 3 rows, ending with a WS row.

Shape shoulder

Cast off 5 sts at beg of next and foll alt row.

Work 1 row.

Cast off rem 5 (6: 6: 6: 6) sts.

RIGHT FRONT

Cast on 61 (65: 67: 71: 73) sts using 2¾mm (US 2) needles and yarn B.

Work as given for back from ★★ to ★★.

Next row (RS): K0 (0: 1: 0: 2), *K2tog, K1, K2tog, rep from * to last 1 (0: 1: 1: 1) sts, K1 (0: 1: 1: 1). 37 (39: 41: 43: 45) sts.

Beg with a **purl** row and working all side seam shaping 2 sts in from ends of rows as given for back, cont in st st, dec 1 st at end of 6th and every foll 4th row until 32 (34: 36: 38: 40) sts rem.

Complete to match left front, reversing shapings.

SLEEVES (both alike)

Cast on 65 (65: 67: 69: 69) sts using 2¾mm (US 2) needles and yarn B.

Work as given for back from ★★ to ★★.

Next row (RS): K0 (0: 1: 2: 2), *K2tog, K1, K2tog, rep from * to last 0 (0: 1: 2: 2) sts, K0 (0: 1: 2: 2). 39 (39: 41: 43: 43) sts.

Beg with a **purl** row and working all sleeve shaping 2 sts in from ends of rows as given for back, cont in st st, shaping sides by inc 1 st at each end of 6th and every foll 14th (12th: 12th: 12th: 10th) row to 43 (45: 49: 51: 57) sts, then on every foll 12th (10th: 10th: 10th: 8th) row until there are 53 (55: 57: 59: 61) sts.

Cont straight until sleeve measures 43 (43: 44: 44: 44) cm **from markers**, ending with a WS row.

Shape top

Cast off 3 (4: 4: 5: 5) sts at beg of next 2 rows. 47 (47: 49: 49: 51) sts.

Dec 1 st at each end of next 3 rows, then on foll 2 alt rows, then on every foll 4th row until 29 (29: 31: 31: 33) sts rem.

Work 1 row.

Dec 1 st at each end of next and every foll alt row until 25 sts rem, then on foll 3 rows, ending with a WS row.

Cast off rem 19 sts.

MAKING UP

PRESS as described on the information page.

Join both shoulder seams using back stitch, or mattress st if preferred.

Neckband

With RS facing, using 3mm (US 2/3) needles and yarn B, pick up and knit 38 (38: 38: 40: 40) sts up right side of neck, 39 (41: 41: 43: 43) sts from back, and 38 (38: 38: 40: 40) sts down left side of neck. 115 (117: 117: 123: 123) sts.

★★★Join in yarn C.

Row 1 (WS): Using yarn C, purl.

Row 2: Using yarn B, knit.

Rows 3 to 10: As rows 1 and 2, 4 times.

Break off yarn C.

Place markers at both ends of last row.

Change to 2¾mm (US 2) needles.

Beg with a P row, work in st st for 12 rows.

Cast off.

Button band

With RS facing, using 3mm (US 2/3) needles and yarn B, pick up and knit 139 (141: 143: 145: 147) sts evenly along left front opening edge between markers on striped borders.

Complete as given for neckband from ★★★.

Buttonhole band

Work as given for button band, making buttonholes in 5th and 17th rows as folls:

Buttonhole row (WS): P2 (3: 4: 2: 3), *P2tog, yrn, P20 (20: 20: 21: 21), rep from * 5 times more, P2tog, yrn, P3 (4: 5: 3: 4).

Leaves (make 2)

Cast on 3 sts using 2¼mm (US 1) needles and yarn D.

Row 1 (RS): K1, (yfwd, K1) twice. 5 sts.

Row 2 and every foll alt row: Purl.

Row 3: K2, yfwd, K1, yfwd, K2. 7 sts.

Row 5: K3, yfwd, K1, yfwd, K3. 9 sts.

Row 7: K4, yfwd, K1, yfwd, K4. 11 sts.

Row 9: K5, yfwd, K1, yfwd, K5. 13 sts.

Rows 11, 13, 15, 17 and 19: Sl 1, K1, psso, K to last 2 sts, K2tog.

Row 21: K3tog and fasten off.

Stem

Cast on 19 sts using 2¼mm (US 1) needles and yarn D.

Knit 1 row.

Cast off.

Flower

Cast on 14 sts using 2¼mm (US 1) needles and waste yarn.

Knit 1 row.

Break off waste yarn and join in yarn E.

Beg with a K row, work in st st for 5 rows.

Break yarn and thread through all 14 sts. Pull up tight and fasten off securely.

Unravel waste yarn and thread end of yarn E left at beg of first row of st st through loops at base of all 14 sts. Pull up tight and fasten off securely. Join row ends of strip, inserting a little washable toy filling if desired.

See information page for finishing instructions, setting in sleeves using the set-in method. Fold first 12 rows to inside around lower edge of body and sleeves and slip stitch in place. Fold neckband in half to inside and slip stitch in place. Fold front bands in half to inside and slip stitch in place. Arrange leaves, stem and flower on left front using photograph as a guide and neatly stitch in place.

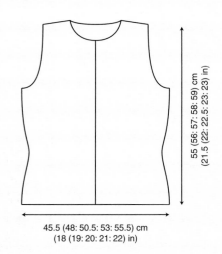

55 (56: 57: 58: 59) cm
(21.5 (22: 22.5: 23: 23) in)

45.5 (48: 50.5: 53: 55.5) cm
(18 (19: 20: 21: 22) in)

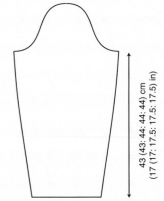

43 (43: 44: 44: 44) cm
(17 (17: 17.5: 17.5: 17.5) in)

COL

SHARON PEAKE

YARN

	XS	S	M	L	XL	
To fit bust	81	86	91	97	102	cm
	32	34	36	38	40	in

Rowan Yorkshire Tweed Chunky

		XS	S	M	L	XL	
A String	551	7	8	8	9	9	x 100gm
B Stout	554	1	1	1	1	1	x 100gm

NEEDLES

1 pair 7mm (no 2) (US 10½) needles
1 pair 8mm (no 0) (US 11) needles

BUTTONS - 6 x 75339

TENSION

14 sts and 23 rows to 10 cm measured over pattern using 8mm (US 11) needles.

BACK

Cast on 59 (63: 67: 71: 75) sts using 7mm (US 10½) needles and yarn A.
Work in garter st for 6 rows, ending with a WS row.
Change to 8mm (US 11) needles.
Row 1 (RS): Knit.
Row 2: Knit.
Row 3: K1, ★slip next st purlwise with yarn at back of work, K1, rep from ★ to end.
Row 4: K1, ★yarn to front, slip next st purlwise with yarn at front of work, yarn to back, K1, rep from ★ to end.
These 4 rows form patt.
Cont in patt, dec 1 st at each end of 5th and every foll 4th row until 49 (53: 57: 61: 65) sts rem.
Work 11 rows, ending with a WS row.
Inc 1 st at each end of next and every foll 8th row until there are 59 (63: 67: 71: 75) sts, taking inc sts into patt.
Cont straight until back measures 36 (37: 37: 38: 38) cm, ending with a WS row.
Shape armholes
Keeping patt correct, cast off 2 (3: 3: 4: 4) sts at beg of next 2 rows. 55 (57: 61: 63: 67) sts.
Dec 1 st at each end of next 1 (1: 3: 3: 5) rows, then on foll 2 alt rows.
49 (51: 51: 53: 53) sts.

Cont straight until armhole measures 19 (19: 20: 20: 21) cm, ending with a WS row.
Shape back neck
Next row (RS): Patt 17 sts and turn, leaving rem sts on a holder.
Work each side of neck separately.
Dec 1 st at neck edge of next 2 rows. 15 sts.
Work 3 rows.
Shape shoulder
Cast off rem 15 sts.
With RS facing, rejoin yarn to rem sts, cast off centre 15 (17: 17: 19: 19) sts, patt to end.
Complete to match first side, reversing shapings.

LEFT FRONT

Cast on 27 (29: 31: 33: 35) sts using 7mm (US 10½) needles and yarn A.
Work in garter st for 6 rows, ending with a WS row.
Change to 8mm (US 11) needles.
Cont in patt as given for back, dec 1 st at beg of 9th and every foll 4th row until 22 (24: 26: 28: 30) sts rem.
Work 11 rows, ending with a WS row.
Inc 1 st at beg of next and every foll 8th row until there are 27 (29: 31: 33: 35) sts, taking inc sts into patt.
Cont straight until left front matches back to beg of armhole shaping, ending with a WS row.
Shape armhole
Keeping patt correct, cast off 2 (3: 3: 4: 4) sts at beg of next row. 25 (26: 28: 29: 31) sts.
Work 1 row.
Shape front slope
Dec 1 st at armhole edge of next 1 (1: 3: 3: 5) rows, then on foll 2 alt rows **and at same time** dec 1 st at front slope edge of next and foll 0 (4th: 6th: 4th: 4th) row. 21 (21: 21: 22: 22) sts.
Dec 1 st at front slope edge of 2nd (6th: 6th: 2nd: 2nd) and every foll 6th (6th: 6th: 4th: 6th) row to 17 (15: 15: 20: 15) sts, then on every foll 8th (-: -: 6th: -) row until 15 (-: -: 15: -) sts rem.
Cont straight until left front matches back to shoulder cast-off, ending with a WS row.
Shape shoulder
Cast off rem 15 sts.

RIGHT FRONT

Cast on 27 (29: 31: 33: 35) sts using 7mm (US 10½) needles and yarn A.
Work in garter st for 6 rows, ending with a WS row.
Change to 8mm (US 11) needles.
Cont in patt as given for back, dec 1 st at end of 9th and every foll 4th row until 22 (24: 26: 28: 30) sts rem.
Complete to match left front, reversing shapings.

SLEEVES (both alike)

Cast on 38 (38: 38: 42: 42) sts using 8mm (US 11) needles and yarn A.
Work in garter st for 4 rows, ending with a WS row.
Work in cuff patt as folls:
Row 1 (RS of cuff): Using yarn A, purl.
Join in yarn B.
Row 2: Using yarn B, K1, ★(K1, P1, K1) all into next st, P3tog, rep from ★ to last st, K1.
Row 3: Using yarn B, purl.
Row 4: Using yarn A, K1, ★P3tog, (K1, P1, K1) all into next st, rep from ★ to last st, K1.
These 2 rows form cuff patt.
Work in cuff patt for a further 8 rows, dec 1 st at each end of next and every foll alt row.
30 (30: 30: 34: 34) sts.
Break off yarn B and cont using yarn A only.

Place markers at both ends of last row.
Change to 7mm (US 10½) needles.
Work in garter st for 5 rows, dec (dec: inc: dec: dec) 1 st at end of last row and ending with WS of cuff, RS of sleeve facing for next row.
29 (29: 31: 33: 33) sts.
Change to 8mm (US 11) needles.
Cont in patt as given for back, shaping sides by inc 1 st at each end of 5th and every foll 6th row to 41 (49: 49: 51: 59) sts, then on every foll 8th row until there are 53 (55: 57: 59: 61) sts, taking inc sts into patt.
Cont straight until sleeve measures 40 (40: 41: 41: 41) cm **from markers**, ending with a WS row.
Shape top
Keeping patt correct, cast off 2 (3: 3: 4: 4) sts at beg of next 2 rows. 49 (49: 51: 51: 53) sts.
Dec 1 st at each end of next and every foll alt row until 23 sts rem.
Work 1 row, ending with a WS row.
Cast off.

MAKING UP

PRESS as described on the information page.
Join both shoulder seams using back stitch, or mattress st if preferred.
Button band
Cast on 6 sts using 7mm (US 10½) needles and yarn A.
Row 1 (RS): Knit.
Row 2: Knit.
Row 3: Purl.
Row 4: Purl.
Rep these 4 rows until band, when slightly stretched, fits up left front opening edge to start of front slope shaping, ending with a WS row.
Cast off.

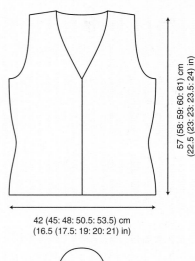

57 (58: 59: 60: 61) cm
(22.5 (23: 23: 23.5: 24) in)

42 (45: 48: 50.5: 53.5) cm
(16.5 (17.5: 19: 20: 21) in)

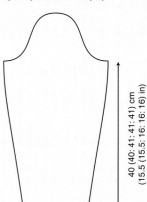

40 (40: 41: 41: 41) cm
(15.5 (15.5: 16: 16: 16) in)

Slip stitch band in place.

Mark positions for 6 buttons on this band – first to come in row 5, last to come 2 cm below start of front slope shaping and rem 4 evenly spaced between.

Buttonhole band

Work to match button band, with the addition of 6 buttonholes worked to correspond with positions marked for buttons as folls:

Buttonhole row (RS): Patt 1 st, work 2 tog, yrn, patt 3 sts.

Slip stitch band in place.

Collar

Cast on 74 (78: 82: 86: 90) sts using 8mm (US 11) needles and yarn A.

Work in garter st for 2 rows, ending with a WS row.

Joining yarn B as required, cont in cuff patt as given for sleeves for 4 rows.

Keeping patt correct, cast off 2 sts at beg of next 26 (28: 30: 30: 32) rows. 22 (22: 22: 26: 26) sts.

Cast off.

Matching row end edges to top of bands, sew shaped cast-off edge of collar to neck edge.

See information page for finishing instructions, setting in sleeves using the set-in method and reversing cuff seam below markers.

Design number 24

BOBBIE

MUIR & OSBORNE

YARN

		XS	S	M	L	XL	
To fit bust		81	86	91	97	102	cm
		32	34	36	38	40	in
Rowan Yorkshire Tweed DK							
A Cheer	343	8	9	9	10	10	x 50gm
B Frolic	350	1	1	1	1	1	x 50gm
C Revel	342	1	1	1	1	1	x 50gm
D Champion	346	1	1	1	1	1	x 50gm
E Lime Leaf	348	1	1	1	1	1	x 50gm
F Frog	349	1	1	1	1	1	x 50gm
G Slosh	345	1	1	1	1	1	x 50gm
H Skip	347	1	1	1	1	1	x 50gm

NEEDLES

1 pair 3¼mm (no 10) (US 3) needles
1 pair 4mm (no 8) (US 6) needles

BUTTONS - 7 x 75321

TENSION

20 sts and 28 rows to 10 cm measured over stocking stitch using 4mm (US 6) needles.

BACK

Cast on 91 (95: 101: 105: 111) sts using 3¼mm (US 3) needles and yarn A.

Row 1 (RS): K1, *P1, K1, rep from * to end.

Row 2: As row 1.

These 2 rows form moss st.

Work in moss st for a further 8 rows, inc 1 st at end of last row and ending with a WS row. 92 (96: 102: 106: 112) sts.

Change to 4mm (US 6) needles.

Using the **intarsia** technique as described on the information page, and starting and ending rows as indicated, cont in patt from chart, which is worked entirely in st st beg with a K row, as folls:

Work 6 rows, ending with a WS row.

Dec 1 st at each end of next and every foll 6th row until 84 (88: 94: 98: 104) sts rem.

Work 15 rows, ending with a WS row.

Inc 1 st at each end of next and every foll 10th row until there are 92 (96: 102: 106: 112) sts, taking inc sts into patt.

Cont straight until chart row 86 (88: 88: 90: 90) has been completed, ending with a WS row. (Work should measure 34 (35: 35: 36: 36) cm.)

Shape armholes

Keeping patt correct, cast off 5 (6: 6: 7: 7) sts at beg of next 2 rows. 82 (84: 90: 92: 98) sts.

Dec 1 st at each end of next 5 (5: 7: 7: 9) rows, then on foll alt row, then on foll 4th row. 68 (70: 72: 74: 76) sts.

Cont straight until chart row 142 (144: 146: 148: 152) has been completed, ending with a WS row. (Armhole should measure 20 (20: 21: 21: 22) cm.)

Shape shoulders and back neck

Cast off 6 (6: 7: 7: 7) sts at beg of next 2 rows. 56 (58: 58: 60: 62) sts.

Next row (RS): Cast off 6 (6: 7: 7: 7) sts, patt until there are 11 (11: 10: 10: 11) sts on right needle and turn, leaving rem sts on a holder.

Work each side of neck separately.

Cast off 4 sts at beg of next row.

Cast off rem 7 (7: 6: 6: 7) sts.

With RS facing, rejoin yarns to rem sts, cast off centre 22 (24: 24: 26: 26) sts, patt to end.

Complete to match first side, reversing shapings.

LEFT FRONT

Cast on 51 (53: 55: 57: 61) sts using 3¼mm (US 3) needles and yarn A.

Work in moss st as given for back for 9 rows, ending with a RS row.

Row 10 (WS): Moss st 6 sts and slip these onto a holder, M1, moss st to last 0 (0: 1: 1: 0) st, (inc in last st) 0 (0: 1: 1: 0) times.
46 (48: 51: 53: 56) sts.

Change to 4mm (US 6) needles.

Starting and ending rows as indicated, cont in patt from chart as folls:

Work 6 rows, ending with a WS row.

Dec 1 st at beg of next and every foll 6th row until 42 (44: 47: 49: 52) sts rem.

Work 15 rows, ending with a WS row.

Inc 1 st at beg of next and every foll 10th row until there are 46 (48: 51: 53: 56) sts, taking inc sts into patt.

Cont straight until left front matches back to beg of armhole shaping, ending with a WS row.

Shape armhole

Keeping patt correct, cast off 5 (6: 6: 7: 7) sts at beg of next row. 41 (42: 45: 46: 49) sts.

Work 1 row.

Dec 1 st at armhole edge of next 5 (5: 7: 7: 9) rows, then on foll alt row, then on foll 4th row. 34 (35: 36: 37: 38) sts.

Cont straight until chart row 125 (127: 129: 129: 133) has been completed, ending with a RS row.

Shape neck

Keeping patt correct, cast off 7 (8: 8: 8: 8) sts at beg of next row.
27 (27: 28: 29: 30) sts.

Dec 1 st at neck edge of next 5 rows, then on foll 2 (2: 2: 3: 3) alt rows, then on foll 4th row.
19 (19: 20: 20: 21) sts.

Work 3 rows, ending with a WS row.

Shape shoulder

Cast off 6 (6: 7: 7: 7) sts at beg of next and foll alt row.

Work 1 row.

Cast off rem 7 (7: 6: 6: 7) sts.

RIGHT FRONT

Cast on 51 (53: 55: 57: 61) sts using 3¼mm (US 3) needles and yarn A.

Work in moss st as given for back for 6 rows, ending with a WS row.

Row 7 (buttonhole row) (RS): K1, P2tog, yrn, moss st to end.

Work in moss st for a further 2 rows, ending with a RS row.

Row 10 (WS): (Inc in first st) 0 (0: 1: 1: 0) times, moss st to last 6 sts, M1 and turn, leaving last 6 sts on a holder.
46 (48: 51: 53: 56) sts.

Change to 4mm (US 6) needles.

Starting and ending rows as indicated, cont in patt from chart as folls:

Work 6 rows, ending with a WS row.

Dec 1 st at end of next and every foll 6th row until 42 (44: 47: 49: 52) sts rem.

Complete to match left front, reversing shapings.

SLEEVES (both alike)

Cast on 45 (45: 47: 49: 49) sts using 3¼mm (US 3) needles and yarn A.

Work in moss st as given for back for 10 rows, inc 1 st at end of last row and ending with a WS row. 46 (46: 48: 50: 50) sts.

Change to 4mm (US 6) needles.

Starting and ending rows as indicated, cont in patt from chart, shaping sides by inc 1 st at each end of 7th and every foll 10th row to 66 (58: 64: 66: 58) sts, then on every foll 8th row until there are 68 (70: 72: 74: 76) sts, taking inc sts into patt.

Cont straight until sleeve measures 46 (46: 47: 47: 47) cm, ending with a WS row.

Shape top

Keeping patt correct, cast off 5 (6: 6: 7: 7) sts at beg of next 2 rows. 58 (58: 60: 60: 62) sts.

Dec 1 st at each end of next 5 rows, then on foll 2 alt rows, then on every foll 4th row until

48 (48: 50: 50: 52) sts rem.

Work 1 row.

Dec 1 st at each end of next and every foll alt row until 40 sts rem, then on foll 3 rows, ending with a WS row. 34 sts.

Cast off 5 sts at beg of next 2 rows.

Cast off rem 24 sts.

MAKING UP

PRESS as described on the information page. Join both shoulder seams using back stitch, or mattress st if preferred.

Button band

Slip 6 sts from left front holder onto 3¼mm (US 3) needles and rejoin yarn A with RS facing.

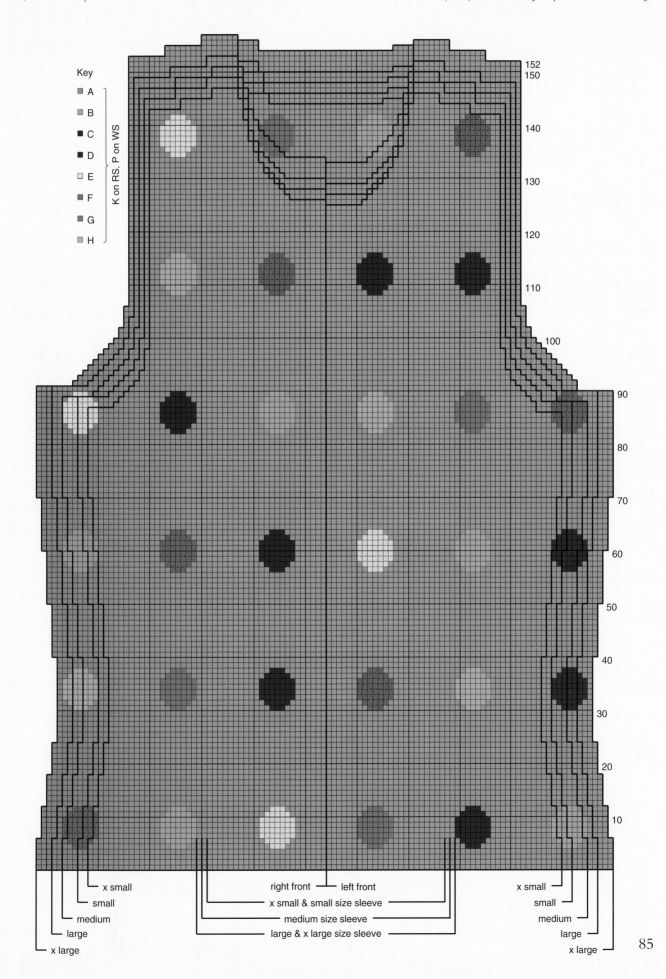

Key

- A
- B
- C
- D
- E
- F
- G
- H

K on RS, P on WS

x small
small
medium
large
x large

right front — left front

x small & small size sleeve
medium size sleeve
large & x large size sleeve

x small
small
medium
large
x large

85

Cont in moss st as set until band, when slightly stretched, fits up left front opening edge to neck shaping, ending with a WS row.
Break yarn and leave sts on a holder.
Slip stitch band in place.
Mark positions for 7 buttons on this band – first to come level with buttonhole already worked in right front, last to come 1 cm above neck shaping and rem 5 evenly spaced between.

Buttonhole band
Slip 6 sts from right front holder onto 3¼mm (US 3) needles and rejoin yarn A with WS facing.
Cont in moss st as set until band, when slightly stretched, fits up right front opening edge to neck shaping, ending with a WS row and with the addition of a further 5 buttonholes worked to correspond with positions marked for buttons as folls:
Buttonhole row (RS): K1, P2tog, yrn (to make a buttonhole), P1, K1, P1.
Do NOT break off yarn.
Slip stitch band in place.

Neckband
With RS facing, using 3¼mm (US 3) needles and yarn A, moss st across 6 sts of buttonhole band, pick up and knit 24 (25: 25: 27: 27) sts up right side of neck, 31 (33: 33: 35: 35) sts from back, and 24 (25: 25: 27: 27) sts down left side of neck, then moss st across 6 sts of button band.
91 (95: 95: 101: 101) sts.
Keeping moss st correct as set by bands, work in moss st for 3 rows, ending with a WS row.
Row 4 (RS): K1, P2tog, yrn (to make 7th buttonhole), moss st to end.
Work in moss st for a further 2 rows.
Cast off in moss st.
See information page for finishing instructions, setting in sleeves using the set-in method.

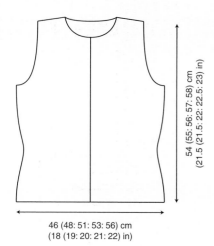

54 (55: 56: 57: 58) cm
(21.5 (21.5: 22: 22.5: 23) in)

46 (48: 51: 53: 56) cm
(18 (19: 20: 21: 22) in)

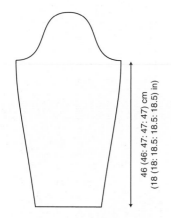

46 (46: 47: 47: 47) cm
(18 (18: 18.5: 18.5: 18.5) in)

HONESTY

KIM HARGREAVES

YARN

	XS	S	M	L	XL	
To fit bust	81	86	91	97	102	cm
	32	34	36	38	40	in
Rowan Yorkshire Tweed DK						
A Lime Leaf 348	10	11	11	12	12	x 50gm
B Frog 349	2	2	2	2	2	x 50gm
C Cheer 343	2	2	2	2	2	x 50gm

NEEDLES
1 pair 3¼mm (no 10) (US 3) needles
1 pair 4mm (no 8) (US 6) needles
Cable needle

BUTTONS - 7 x 75321

TENSION
22½ sts and 28 rows to 10 cm measured over pattern using 4mm (US 6) needles.

SPECIAL ABBREVIATIONS
C4F = Cable 4 front Slip next 2 sts onto cable needle and leave at front of work, K2, then K2 from cable needle
C4B = Cable 4 back Slip next 2 sts onto cable needle and leave at back of work, K2, then K2 from cable needle
MB = Make bobble Using yarn C, K into front, back, front, back and front again of next st, turn, P5, turn, slip 2 sts, K3tog, pass 2 slipped sts over

BACK
Cast on 107 (113: 119: 125: 131) sts using 3¼mm (US 3) needles and yarn A.
Row 1 (RS): Knit.
Row 2: P0 (1: 0: 0: 0), K0 (2: 2: 1: 0), (P2, K2) 1 (1: 2: 3: 4) times, ★P4, K2, P2, K2, P3, K2, P2, K2, rep from ★ to last 8 (11: 14: 17: 20) sts, P4, (K2, P2) 1 (1: 2: 3: 4) times, K0 (2: 2: 1: 0), P0 (1: 0: 0: 0).
These 2 rows form rib.
Work in rib for a further 6 rows, ending with a WS row.
Change to 4mm (US 6) needles.
Using the **intarsia** technique as described on

the information page, starting and ending rows as indicated and repeating the 8 row pattern repeat throughout, cont in patt from chart as folls:
Work 8 rows, ending with a WS row.
Dec 1 st at each end of next and every foll 4th row until 95 (101: 107: 113: 119) sts rem.
Work 9 rows, ending with a WS row.
Inc 1 st at each end of next and every foll 8th row until there are 107 (113: 119: 125: 131) sts, taking inc sts into patt.
Cont straight until back measures 33 (34: 34: 35: 35) cm, ending with a WS row.
Shape armholes
Keeping patt correct, cast off 4 (5: 5: 6: 6) sts at beg of next 2 rows. 99 (103: 109: 113: 119) sts.
Dec 1 st at each end of next 5 (5: 7: 7: 9) rows, then on foll 2 (3: 3: 4: 4) alt rows.
85 (87: 89: 91: 93) sts.
Cont straight until armhole measures 20 (20: 21: 21: 22) cm, ending with a WS row.
Shape shoulders and back neck
Cast off 9 sts at beg of next 2 rows.
67 (69: 71: 73: 75) sts.
Next row (RS): Cast off 9 sts, patt until there are 12 (12: 13: 13: 14) sts on right needle and turn, leaving rem sts on a holder.
Work each side of neck separately.
Cast off 4 sts at beg of next row.
Cast off rem 8 (8: 9: 9: 10) sts.
With RS facing, rejoin yarns to rem sts, cast off centre 25 (27: 27: 29: 29) sts, patt to end.
Complete to match first side, reversing shapings.

LEFT FRONT
Cast on 57 (60: 63: 66: 69) sts using 3¼mm (US 3) needles and yarn A.
Row 1 (RS): K to last 5 sts, (P1, K1) twice, P1.
Row 2: (P1, K1) 3 times, P3, K2, (P4, K2, P2, K2, P3, K2, P2, K2) twice, P4, (K2, P2) 1 (1: 2: 3: 4) times, K0 (2: 2: 1: 0), P0 (1: 0: 0: 0).
These 2 rows set the sts – front opening edge 6 sts in moss st with all other sts in rib.
Cont as set for a further 5 rows, ending with a RS row.
Row 8 (WS): Moss st 6 sts and slip these 6 sts onto a holder, M1, rib to end.
52 (55: 58: 61: 64) sts.
Change to 4mm (US 6) needles.
Starting and ending rows as indicated, cont in patt from chart as folls:
(**Note:** do **NOT** work part motifs along front opening edge.)
Work 8 rows, ending with a WS row.
Dec 1 st at beg of next and every foll 4th row until 46 (49: 52: 55: 58) sts rem.
Work 9 rows, ending with a WS row.
Inc 1 st at beg of next and every foll 8th row until there are 52 (55: 58: 61: 64) sts, taking inc sts into patt.
Cont straight until left front matches back to beg of armhole shaping, ending with a WS row.
Shape armhole
Keeping patt correct, cast off 4 (5: 5: 6: 6) sts at beg of next row. 48 (50: 53: 55: 58) sts.
Work 1 row.
Dec 1 st at armhole edge of next 5 (5: 7: 7: 9) rows, then on foll 2 (3: 3: 4: 4) alt rows.
41 (42: 43: 44: 45) sts.
Cont straight until 17 (17: 17: 19: 19) rows less have been worked than on back to start of shoulder shaping, ending with a RS row.
Shape neck
Keeping patt correct, cast off 5 (6: 6: 6: 6) sts at beg of next row.
36 (36: 37: 38: 39) sts.

Dec 1 st at neck edge of next 6 rows, then on foll 4 (4: 4: 5: 5) alt rows. 26 (26: 27: 27: 28) sts.
Work 2 rows, ending with a WS row.

Shape shoulder
Cast off 9 sts at beg of next and foll alt row.
Work 1 row.
Cast off rem 8 (8: 9: 9: 10) sts.

RIGHT FRONT
Cast on 57 (60: 63: 66: 69) sts using 3¼mm (US 3) needles and yarn A.

Row 1 (RS): P1, (K1, P1) twice, K to end.
Row 2: P0 (1: 0: 0: 0), K0 (2: 2: 1: 0), (P2, K2) 1 (1: 2: 3: 4) times, (P4, K2, P2, K2, P3, K2, P2, K2) twice, P4, K2, P3, (K1, P1) 3 times.
These 2 rows set the sts – front opening edge 6 sts in moss st with all other sts in rib.
Cont as set for a further 2 rows, ending with a WS row.
Row 5 (RS): P1, K2tog, yfwd (to make first buttonhole), patt to end.
Work a further 2 rows, ending with a RS row.
Row 8 (WS): Rib to last 6 sts, M1 and turn, leaving rem 6 sts on a holder.
52 (55: 58: 61: 64) sts.
Change to 4mm (US 6) needles.
Starting and ending rows as indicated, cont in patt from chart as folls:
(**Note**: do **NOT** work part motifs along front opening edge.)
Work 8 rows, ending with a WS row.
Dec 1 st at end of next and every foll 4th row until 46 (49: 52: 55: 58) sts rem.
Complete to match left front, reversing shapings.

SLEEVES (both alike)
Cast on 63 (63: 65: 67: 67) sts using 3¼mm (US 3) needles and yarn A.
Row 1 (RS): Knit.
Row 2: P0 (0: 0: 1: 1), K1 (1: 2: 2: 2), (P4, K2, P2, K2, P3, K2, P2, K2) 3 times, P4, K1 (1: 2: 2: 2), P0 (0: 0: 1: 1).
These 2 rows form rib.
Work in rib for a further 6 rows, ending with a WS row.
Change to 4mm (US 6) needles.
Starting and ending rows as indicated, cont in patt from chart, shaping sides by inc 1 st at each end of 13th (11th: 11th: 11th: 9th) and every foll 14th (12th: 12th: 12th: 12th) row to 73 (73: 71: 73: 85) sts, then on every foll 16th (14th: 14th: 14th: -) row until there are 77 (79: 81: 83: -) sts, taking inc sts into patt.
Cont straight until sleeve measures 43 (43: 44: 44: 44) cm, ending with a WS row.

Shape top
Keeping patt correct, cast off 4 (5: 5: 6: 6) sts at beg of next 2 rows. 69 (69: 71: 71: 73) sts.
Dec 1 st at each end of next 3 rows, then on foll 2 alt rows, then on every foll 4th row until 47 (47: 49: 49: 51) sts rem.
Work 1 row.
Dec 1 st at each end of next and every foll alt row until 43 sts rem, then on foll row, ending with a WS row. 41 sts.
Cast off 4 sts at beg of next 2 rows.
Cast off rem 33 sts.

MAKING UP
PRESS as described on the information page.
Join both shoulder seams using back stitch, or mattress st if preferred.
Button band
Slip 6 sts from left front holder onto 3¼mm (US 3) needles and rejoin yarn A with RS facing.

Cont in moss st as set until band, when slightly stretched, fits up left front opening edge to neck shaping.
Cast off.
Slip stitch band in place.
Mark positions for 7 buttons on this band – first to come level with buttonhole already worked in right front, last to come 1 cm down from neck shaping and rem 5 evenly spaced between.
Buttonhole band
Slip 6 sts from right front holder onto 3¼mm (US 3) needles and rejoin yarn A with WS facing.
Cont in moss st as set until band, when slightly stretched, fits up left front opening edge to neck shaping with the addition of a further 6 buttonholes worked to correspond with positions marked for buttons as folls:
Buttonhole row (RS): P1, K2tog, yfwd (to make a buttonhole), moss st to end.
Slip stitch band in place.
Collar
Cast on 91 (91: 91: 101: 101) sts using 3¼mm (US 3) needles and yarn A.
Row 1 (RS): K1, *P1, K1, rep from * to end.
Row 2: As row 1.
These 2 rows form moss st.
Work in moss st for a further 4 rows, ending with a WS row.
Using the **intarsia** technique as described on the information page, starting and ending rows as indicated and repeating the 10 st pattern repeat 6 (6: 6: 7: 7) times, cont in patt from chart for collar until all 32 rows have been completed, ending with a WS row.
Cast off.
Placing ends of collar halfway across top of front bands, sew cast-off edge of collar to neck edge.
See information page for finishing instructions, setting in sleeves using the set-in method.

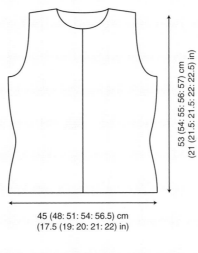

45 (48: 51: 54: 56.5) cm
(17.5 (19: 20: 21: 22) in)

53 (54: 55: 56: 57) cm
(21 (21.5: 21.5: 22: 22.5) in)

43 (43: 44: 44: 44) cm
(17 (17: 17.5: 17.5: 17.5) in)

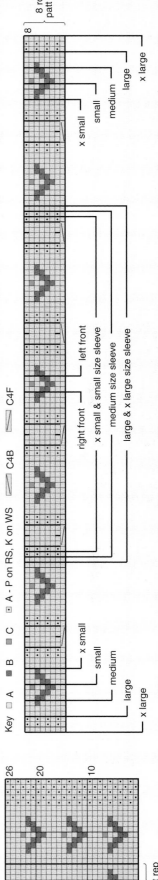

8 row patt rep

8

x large
large
medium
small
x small

left front

right front

x small & small size sleeve

medium size sleeve

large & x large size sleeve

x small
small
medium
large
x large

Key ☐ A ■ B ▨ C ⊡ A - P on RS, K on WS ╱ C4B ╱ C4F

Collar chart

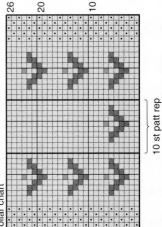

26

20

10

10 st patt rep

SAMPLER

KIM HARGREAVES

YARN

		XS	S	M	L	XL	
To fit bust		81	86	91	97	102	cm
		32	34	36	38	40	in

Rowan Yorkshire Tweed 4 ply

A Barley	264	11	11	12	12	13	x 25gm
B Shrew	265	1	1	1	1	1	x 25gm
C Highlander	266	2	2	2	2	2	x 25gm
D Sheer	267	2	2	2	2	2	x 25gm
E Stainless	270	1	1	1	1	1	x 25gm
F Explode	277	1	1	1	1	1	x 25gm
G Radiant	276	1	1	1	1	1	x 25gm
H Enchant	268	1	1	1	1	1	x 25gm
J Blessed	269	1	1	2	2	2	x 25gm

NEEDLES

1 pair 2¾mm (no 12) (US 2) needles
1 pair 3¼mm (no 10) (US 3) needles

BUTTONS - 7 x 75320

TENSION

30 sts and 35 rows to 10 cm measured over patterned stocking stitch using 3¼mm (US 3) needles.

BACK

Cast on 121 (129: 137: 145: 153) sts using 2¾mm (US 2) needles and yarn D.
Break off yarn D and join in yarn A.
Row 1 (RS): K1, *P1, K1, rep from * to end.
Row 2: P1, *K1, P1, rep from * to end.
These 2 rows form rib.
Cont in rib until back measures 6 cm, ending with a WS row.
Change to 3¼mm (US 3) needles.
Using the **fairisle** technique as described on the information page and starting and ending rows as indicated, cont in patt from chart for back and fronts, which is worked entirely in st st as folls:
Inc 1 st at each end of 3rd and every foll 10th row until there are 137 (145: 153: 161: 169) sts, taking inc sts into patt.
Cont straight until chart row 86 (90: 90: 94: 94) has been completed, ending with a WS row.
(Back should measure 31 (32: 32: 33: 33) cm.)

Shape armholes

Keeping chart correct, cast off 5 (6: 6: 7: 7) sts at beg of next 2 rows. 127 (133: 141: 147: 155) sts.
Dec 1 st at each end of next 7 (7: 9: 9: 11) rows, then on foll 4 (5: 5: 6: 6) alt rows.
105 (109: 113: 117: 121) sts.
Cont straight until chart row 156 (160: 164: 168: 172) has been completed, ending with a WS row.
(Armhole should measure 20 (20: 21: 21: 22) cm.)

Shape shoulders and back neck

Cast off 10 (11: 11: 12: 12) sts at beg of next 2 rows. 85 (87: 91: 93: 97) sts.
Next row (RS): Cast off 10 (11: 11: 12: 12) sts, patt until there are 15 (14: 16: 15: 17) sts on right needle and turn, leaving rem sts on a holder.
Work each side of neck separately.
Cast off 4 sts at beg of next row.
Cast off rem 11 (10: 12: 11: 13) sts.
With RS facing, rejoin yarns to rem sts, cast off centre 35 (37: 37: 39: 39) sts, patt to end.
Complete to match first side, reversing shapings.

LEFT FRONT

Cast on 66 (70: 74: 78: 82) sts using 2¾mm (US 2) needles and yarn D.
Break off yarn D and join in yarn A.
Row 1 (RS): *K1, P1, rep from * to last 2 sts, K2.
Row 2: *K1, P1, rep from * to end.
These 2 rows form rib.
Cont in rib until left front measures 6 cm, ending with a **RS** row.
Next row (WS): Rib 7 and slip these 7 sts onto a holder, M1, rib to last st, inc in last st. 61 (65: 69: 73: 77) sts.
Change to 3¼mm (US 3) needles.
Starting and ending rows as indicated, cont in patt from chart for back and fronts as folls:
Inc 1 st at beg of 3rd and every foll 10th row until there are 69 (73: 77: 81: 85) sts, taking inc sts into patt.
Cont straight until left front matches back to beg of armhole shaping, ending with a WS row.

Shape armhole

Keeping chart correct, cast off 5 (6: 6: 7: 7) sts at beg of next row. 64 (67: 71: 74: 78) sts.
Work 1 row.
Dec 1 st at armhole edge of next 7 (7: 9: 9: 11) rows, then on foll 4 (5: 5: 6: 6) alt rows.
53 (55: 57: 59: 61) sts.
Cont straight until chart row 133 (137: 141: 143: 147) has been completed, ending with a RS row.

Shape neck

Keeping chart correct, cast off 9 (10: 10: 10: 10) sts at beg of next row.
44 (45: 47: 49: 51) sts.
Dec 1 st at neck edge of next 10 rows, then on foll 3 (3: 3: 4: 4) alt rows. 31 (32: 34: 35: 37) sts.

Work 6 rows, ending after chart row 156 (160: 164: 168: 172) and with a WS row.

Shape shoulder

Cast off 10 (11: 11: 12: 12) sts at beg of next and foll alt row.
Work 1 row.
Cast off rem 11 (10: 12: 11: 13) sts.

RIGHT FRONT

Cast on 66 (70: 74: 78: 82) sts using 2¾mm (US 2) needles and yarn D.
Break off yarn D and join in yarn A.
Row 1 (RS): K2, *P1, K1, rep from * to end.
Row 2: *P1, K1, rep from * to end.
These 2 rows form rib.
Work in rib for a further 2 rows.

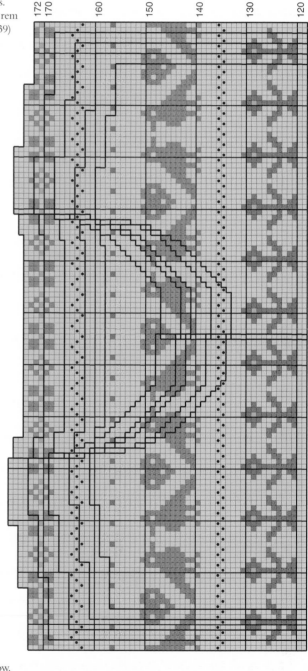

Key
A B C D E F G H J

Row 5 (buttonhole row) (RS): Rib 2, work 2 tog, yrn, rib to end.
Cont in rib until right front measures 6 cm, ending with a **RS** row.
Next row (WS): Inc in first st, rib to last 7 sts, M1 and turn, leaving last 7 sts on a holder. 61 (65: 69: 73: 77) sts.

Change to 3¼mm (US 3) needles.
Starting and ending rows as indicated, cont in patt from chart for back and fronts as folls:
Inc 1 st at end of 3rd and every foll 10th row until there are 69 (73: 77: 81: 85) sts, taking inc sts into patt.
Complete to match left front, reversing shapings.

SLEEVES (both alike)
Cast on 83 (83: 85: 87: 87) sts using 2¾mm (US 2) needles and yarn D.
Break off yarn D and join in yarn A.
Work in rib as given for back for 6 cm, ending with a WS row.
Change to 3¼mm (US 3) needles.

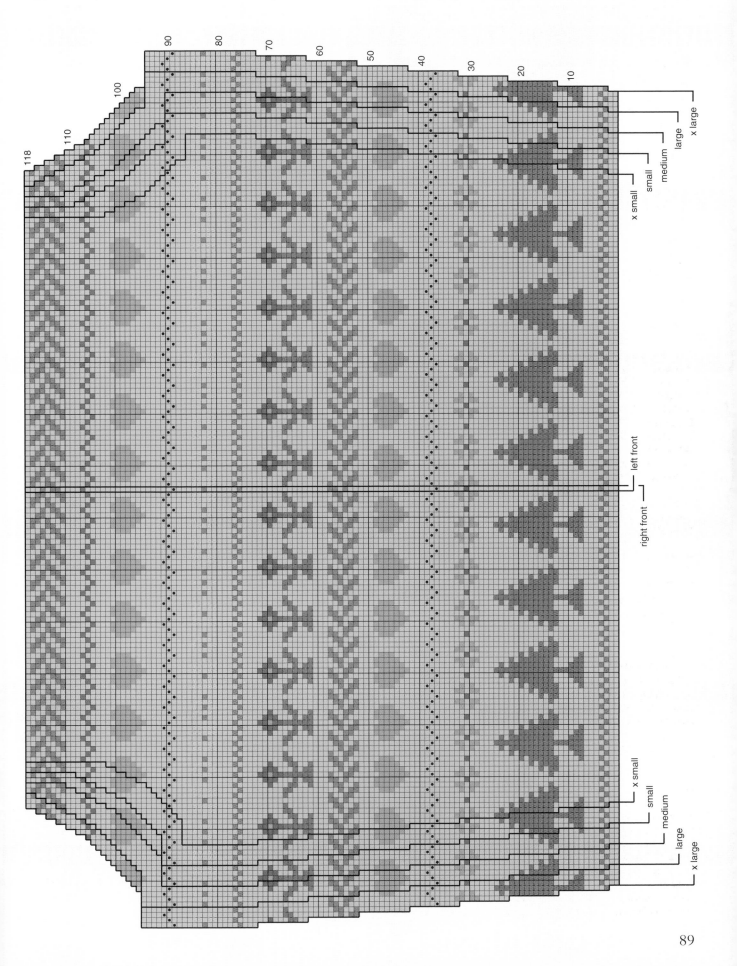

89

x small & small size sleeve

medium size sleeve

large & x large size sleeve

Using the **fairisle** technique as described on the information page and starting and ending rows as indicated, cont in patt from chart for sleeves, which is worked entirely in st st beg with a K row, as folls:
Inc 1 st at each end of 3rd and every foll 14th (14th: 12th: 12th: 10th) row to 95 (87: 97: 103: 107) sts, then on every foll 12th (12th: 10th: 10th: 8th) row until there are 101 (103: 107: 109: 113) sts, taking inc sts into patt.
Cont straight until chart row 126 (130: 130: 134: 134) has been completed, ending with a WS row. (Sleeve should measure 42 (43: 43: 44: 44) cm.)
Shape top
Keeping chart correct, cast off 5 (6: 6: 7: 7) sts at beg of next 2 rows.
91 (91: 95: 95: 99) sts.
Dec 1 st at each end of next 5 rows, then on foll 4 alt rows, then on every foll 4th row until 63 (63: 67: 67: 71) sts rem.
Work 1 row.
Dec 1 st at each end of next and every foll alt row until
55 sts rem, then on foll 5 rows, ending with a WS row.
Cast off 4 sts at beg of next 2 rows.
Cast off rem 37 sts.

MAKING UP
PRESS as described on the information page.
Join both shoulder seams using back stitch, or mattress st if preferred.
Button band
Slip 7 sts from left front holder onto 2¾mm (US 2) needles and rejoin yarn A with RS facing.
Cont in rib as set until band, when slightly stretched, fits up left front opening edge to neck shaping, ending with a WS row.
Break yarn and leave sts on a holder.
Slip stitch band in place.

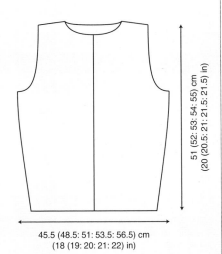

51 (52: 53: 54: 55) cm
(20 (20.5: 21: 21.5: 21.5) in)

45.5 (48.5: 51: 53.5: 56.5) cm
(18 (19: 20: 21: 22) in)

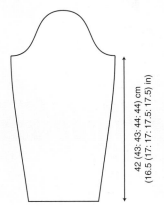

42 (43: 43: 44: 44) cm
(16.5 (17: 17: 17.5: 17.5) in)

Mark positions for 7 buttons on this band – first to come level with buttonhole already worked in right front, second to come 7 cm up from cast-on edge, last to come just above neck shaping and rem 4 evenly spaced between.
Buttonhole band
Slip 7 sts from right front holder onto 2¾mm (US 2) needles and rejoin yarn A with WS facing.
Cont in rib as set until band, when slightly stretched, fits up right front opening edge to neck shaping, ending with a WS row and with the addition of a further 5 buttonholes worked to correspond with positions marked for buttons as folls:
Buttonhole row (RS): Rib 2, work 2 tog, yrn, rib 3.
Do NOT break yarn.

Design number 27

PERKINS

SARAH DALLAS

YARN

		XS	S	M	L	XL	
To fit bust		81	86	91	97	102	cm
		32	34	36	38	40	in
Rowan Yorkshire Tweed DK							
A Frog	349	4	5	5	5	5	x 50gm
B Revel	342	2	2	2	2	2	x 50gm
C Skip	347	2	2	2	2	2	x 50gm
D Frolic	350	3	3	3	3	3	x 50gm
E Scarlet	344	2	2	2	2	2	x 50gm

NEEDLES
1 pair 3¼mm (no 10) (US 3) needles
1 pair 4mm (no 8) (US 6) needles
3.50mm (no 9) (US E4) crochet hook

BUTTONS - 7 x 75320

TENSION
20 sts and 28 rows to 10 cm measured over stocking stitch using 4mm (US 6) needles.

STRIPE SEQUENCE
Rows 1 to 6: Using yarn A.
Row 7: Using yarn B.
Row 8: Using yarn C.

Row 9: Using yarn B.
Rows 10 to 15: Using yarn D.
Rows 16 to 18: As rows 7 to 9.
These 18 rows form stripe sequence.

BACK
Cast on 95 (99: 105: 109: 115) sts using 4mm (US 6) needles and yarn A.
Row 1 (RS): K2 (4: 0: 1: 4), P1 (1: 0: 1: 1), K1, P1, *K5, P1, K1, P1, rep from * to last 2 (4: 7: 1: 4) sts, K2 (4: 5: 1: 4), P0 (0: 1: 0: 0), K0 (0: 1: 0: 0).
Row 2: P2 (4: 0: 1: 4), K1 (1: 0: 1: 1), P1, K1, *P5, K1, P1, K1, rep from * to last 2 (4: 7: 1: 4) sts, P2 (4: 5: 1: 4), K0 (0: 1: 0: 0), P0 (0: 1: 0: 0).
These 2 rows form rib.
Starting with a further 4 rows using yarn A, cont in rib in stripe sequence as given above until back measures 26 (27: 27: 28: 28) cm, ending with a WS row.
Shape armholes
Keeping striped rib correct, cast off 6 sts at beg of next 2 rows. 83 (87: 93: 97: 103) sts.
Dec 1 st at each end of next 3 rows.
77 (81: 87: 91: 97) sts.
Cont straight until armhole measures 20 (20: 21: 21: 22) cm, ending with a WS row.
Shape shoulders and back neck
Cast off 8 (8: 9: 9: 10) sts at beg of next 2 rows.
61 (65: 69: 73: 77) sts.
Next row (RS): Cast off 8 (8: 9: 9: 10) sts, rib until there are 11 (12: 13: 14: 15) sts on right needle and turn, leaving rem sts on a holder.
Work each side of neck separately.
Cast off 4 sts at beg of next row.
Cast off rem 7 (8: 9: 10: 11) sts.
With RS facing, rejoin appropriate yarn to rem sts, cast off centre 23 (25: 25: 27: 27) sts, rib to end.
Complete to match first side, reversing shapings.

LEFT FRONT
Cast on 48 (50: 53: 55: 58) sts using 4mm (US 6) needles and yarn A.
Row 1 (RS): K2 (4: 0: 1: 4), P1 (1: 0: 1: 1), K1, P1, *K5, P1, K1, P1, rep from * to last 3 sts, K3.
Row 2: P3, K1, P1, K1, *P5, K1, P1, K1, rep from * to last 2 (4: 7: 1: 4) sts, P2 (4: 5: 1: 4), K0 (0: 1: 0: 0), P0 (0: 1: 0: 0).
These 2 rows form rib.
Starting with a further 4 rows using yarn A, cont in rib in stripe sequence as given above until left front matches back to beg of armhole shaping, ending with a WS row.
Shape armhole
Keeping striped rib correct, cast off 6 sts at beg of next row. 42 (44: 47: 49: 52) sts.

Slip stitch band in place.
Neckband
With RS facing, using 2¾mm (US 2) needles and yarn A, rib across 7 sts from right front holder, pick up and knit 34 (35: 35: 37: 37) sts up right side of neck, 43 (45: 45: 47: 47) sts from back, and 34 (35: 35: 37: 37) sts down left side of neck, then rib across 7 sts from left front holder.
125 (129: 129: 135: 135) sts.
Keeping rib correct as set by bands, work in rib for 3 rows, ending with a WS row.
Row 4 (RS): Rib 2, work 2 tog, yrn (to make 7th buttonhole), rib to end.
Work in rib for a further 4 rows.
Cast off in rib (on WS).
See information page for finishing instructions, setting in sleeves using the set-in method.

Work 1 row.

Dec 1 st at armhole edge of next 3 rows.
39 (41: 44: 46: 49) sts.

Cont straight until 15 (15: 15: 17: 17) rows less
have been worked than on back to start of
shoulder shaping, ending with a RS row.

Shape neck

Keeping patt correct, cast off 9 (10: 10: 10: 10) sts
at beg of next row. 30 (31: 34: 36: 39) sts.

Dec 1 st at neck edge of next 3 rows, then on
foll 3 (3: 3: 4: 4) alt rows, then on foll 4th row.
23 (24: 27: 28: 31) sts.

Work 1 row, ending with a WS row.

Shape shoulder

Cast off 8 (8: 9: 9: 10) sts at beg of next and foll
alt row.

Work 1 row. Cast off rem 7 (8: 9: 10: 11) sts.

RIGHT FRONT

Cast on 48 (50: 53: 55: 58) sts using 4mm (US 6)
needles and yarn A.

Row 1 (RS): K3, P1, K1, P1, ★K5, P1, K1, P1,
rep from ★ to last 2 (4: 7: 1: 4) sts, K2 (4: 5: 1: 4),
P0 (0: 1: 0: 0), K0 (0: 1: 0: 0).

Row 2: P2 (4: 0: 1: 4), K1 (1: 0: 1: 1), P1, K1,
★P5, K1, P1, K1, rep from ★ to last 3 sts, P3.

These 2 rows form rib.

Work to match left front, reversing shapings.

SLEEVES (both alike)

Cast on 48 (48: 50: 52: 52) sts using 4mm (US 6)
needles and yarn A.

Beg with a K row and 6 rows using yarn A,
cont in st st in stripe sequence as given above,
shaping sides by inc 1 st at each end of 7th (7th:
5th: 7th: 5th) and every foll 6th (6th: 6th: 6th:
4th) row to 78 (78: 84: 80: 60) sts, then on every
foll 8th (8th: –: 8th: 6th) row until there are
80 (80: –: 84: 88) sts.

Cont straight until sleeve measures 40 (40: 41:
41: 41) cm, ending with a WS row.

Shape top

Keeping stripes correct, cast off 6 sts at beg of
next 2 rows. 68 (68: 72: 72: 76) sts.

Dec 1 st at each end of next and foll 2 alt rows,
then on foll row, ending with a WS row.

Cast off rem 60 (60: 64: 64: 68) sts.

MAKING UP

PRESS as described on the information page.

Crochet vertical stripes

With RS facing, 3.50mm (US E4) crochet hook
and yarn E, work in chain st up each P st ridge
of rib on back and fronts as folls: with yarn at
WS of work, insert hook into st at base of P st
ridge and draw loop through, ★insert hook
through next st above and draw loop through this
st and loop on hook, rep from ★ to cast-off edge.
Join both shoulder seams using back stitch, or
mattress st if preferred.

Button band

With RS facing, using 3¼mm (US 3) needles
and yarn A, pick up and knit 92 (92: 96: 96: 96)
sts evenly down left front opening edge, between
neck shaping and cast-on edge.

Row 1 (WS): K1, ★P2, K2, rep from ★ to last
3 sts, P2, K1.

Row 2: K3, ★P2, K2, rep from ★ to last st, K1.

These 2 rows form rib.

Work in rib for a further 4 rows.

Cast off in rib (on WS).

Buttonhole band

Work to match button band, picking up sts up
right front opening edge and with the addition
of 6 buttonholes worked in row 4 as folls:

Row 4 (RS): Rib 3 (3: 2: 2: 2), ★yrn, work 2
tog tbl (to make a buttonhole), rib 14 (14: 15: 15:
15) rep from ★ to last 9 sts, yrn, work 2 tog tbl
(to make 6th buttonhole), rib to end.

Neckband

With RS facing, using 3¼mm (US 3) needles
and yarn A, starting and ending at cast-off edge
of bands, pick up and knit 26 (27: 27: 30: 30) sts
up right side of neck, 32 (34: 34: 36: 36) sts from
back, then 26 (27: 27: 30: 30) sts down left side
of neck. 84 (88: 88: 96: 96) sts.

Work in rib as given for button band for 3 rows.

Row 4 (RS): Rib 3, work 2 tog tbl, yrn (to
make 7th buttonhole), rib to end.

Work a further 2 rows. Cast off in rib (on WS).
Join side seams.

Lace edging

Cast on 13 sts using 3¼mm (US 3) needles and
yarn A.

Row 1 and every foll alt row: K2, P to last
2 sts, K2.

Row 2: K7, yfwd, sl 1, K1, psso, yfwd, K4. 14 sts.

Row 4: K6, (yfwd, sl 1, K1, psso) twice, yfwd, K4.
15 sts.

Row 6: K5, (yfwd, sl 1, K1, psso) 3 times, yfwd,
K4. 16 sts.

Row 8: K4, (yfwd, sl 1, K1, psso) 4 times, yfwd,
K4. 17 sts.

Row 10: K3, (yfwd, sl 1, K1, psso) 5 times, yfwd,
K4. 18 sts.

Row 12: K4, (yfwd, sl 1, K1, psso) 5 times,
K2tog, K2. 17 sts.

Row 14: K5, (yfwd, sl 1, K1, psso) 4 times,
K2tog, K2. 16 sts.

Row 16: K6, (yfwd, sl 1, K1, psso) 3 times,
K2tog, K2. 15 sts.

Row 18: K7, (yfwd, sl 1, K1, psso) twice, K2tog,
K2. 14 sts.

Row 20: K8, yfwd, sl 1, K1, psso, K2tog, K2. 13 sts.

These 20 rows form patt.

Cont in patt until lace edging fits along entire
lower edge of back and fronts, ending with row 20.
Cast off.

Slip st lace edging in place.

In same way, make and attach lace edging to
cast-on edge of sleeves.

See information page for finishing instructions,
setting in sleeves using the shallow set-in method.

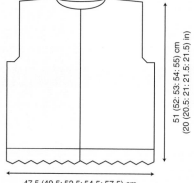

47.5 (49.5: 52.5: 54.5: 57.5) cm
(18.5 (19.5: 20.5: 21.5: 22.5) in)

51 (52: 53: 54: 55) cm
(20 (20.5: 21: 21.5: 21.5) in)

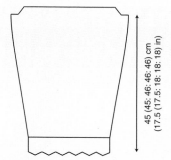

45 (45: 46: 46: 46) cm
(17.5 (17.5: 18: 18: 18) in)

Design number 28

SAILOR STRIPE

KIM HARGREAVES

YARN

		XS	S	M	L	XL	
To fit bust		81	86	91	97	102	cm
		32	34	36	38	40	in

Rowan Yorkshire Tweed 4 ply

A Dessicated	263	11	11	12	13	13	x 25gm
B Sheer	267	2	2	2	2	2	x 25gm

NEEDLES

1 pair 2¾mm (no 12) (US 2) needles
1 pair 3mm (no 11) (US 2/3) needles
1 pair 3¼mm (no 10) (US 3) needles

TENSION

26 sts and 38 rows to 10 cm measured over
stocking stitch using 3¼mm (US 3) needles.

BACK

Cast on 118 (124: 130: 138: 144) sts using 2¾mm
(US 2) needles and yarn B.

★★Beg with a K row, work in st st for 12 rows,
ending with a WS row.

Place markers at both ends of last row.

Change to 3mm (US 2/3) needles.

Join in yarn A.

Row 13 (RS): Using yarn A, knit.

Row 14: Using yarn B, purl.

Rows 15 to 22: As rows 13 and 14, 4 times.

Break off yarn B and cont using yarn A **only**.

Change to 3¼mm (US 3) needles.★★

Beg with a K row, cont in st st until back
measures 30 (31: 31: 32: 32) cm **from markers**,
ending with a WS row.

Shape armholes

Cast off 5 (6: 6: 7: 7) sts at beg of next 2 rows.
108 (112: 118: 124: 130) sts.★★★

Dec 1 st at each end of next 5 (5: 7: 7: 9) rows, then
on foll 5 (6: 6: 7: 7) alt rows. 88 (90: 92: 96: 98) sts.

Cont straight until armhole measures 20 (20: 21:
21: 22) cm, ending with a WS row.

Shape shoulders and back neck

Cast off 8 (8: 9: 9: 9) sts at beg of next 2 rows.
72 (74: 74: 78: 80) sts.

Next row (RS): Cast off 8 (8: 9: 9: 9) sts, K
until there are 13 (13: 12: 13: 14) sts on right
needle and turn, leaving rem sts on a holder.